JOHN FOWLES

MODERN LITERATURE MONOGRAPHS

GENERAL EDITOR: Lina Mainiero

(Continued on last page of book)

JOHN FOWLES

Barry N. Olshen

FREDERICK UNGAR PUBLISHING CO.
NEW YORK

Copyright © 1978 by Frederick Ungar Publishing Co., Inc.
Printed in the United States of America
Design by Anita Duncan

Library of Congress Cataloging in Publication Data
Olshen, Barry N.
    John Fowles.
    (Modern literature monographs)
    Bibliography: p.
    Includes index.
    1. Fowles, John, 1926-   —Criticism and interpre-
tation.
PR6056.085Z79   1978   823'.9'14   78-3419
ISBN 0-8044-2655-1

Second Printing, 1979

For Toni and Jessica

Acknowledgments

It is a pleasure to express my sincere gratitude to those who have helped in the creation of this book: to my wife, Toni, who shared every stage of its development from the initial proposal to the final proofs, and who helped with the research, the bibliography, and the index; to John Fowles for his hospitality and encouragement, and for his kind attention to the manuscript; to my friend and colleague, Anthony Hopkins, who read parts of the manuscript and offered much valuable criticism; to the librarians of the Frost Library, Glendon College, for their willing and diligent attention to my research needs; and to York University for research grants to defray expenses while at work on the manuscript.

Contents

Chronology

1926	31 March: John Fowles is born in Leigh-on-Sea, Essex, England, to Gladys (nee Richards) and Robert J. Fowles.
1940–44	Attends Bedford School.
1944	Attends the University of Edinburgh for six months.
1945–46	Serves one and one-half years as a lieutenant in the Royal Marines.
1947–50	Studies French at New College, Oxford University; receives BA (Honors), 1950.
1950–51	*Lecteur* (reader) in English at the University of Poitiers, France.
1951–52	Teaches English at Anargyrios College, Spetsai, Greece.
1953–63	Assumes various teaching posts in and around London: his last position as head of the English Department, St. Godric's, Hampstead.
1956	Marries Elizabeth Whitton.
1963	*The Collector* is published.
1964	*The Aristos* is published.
1965	*The Magus* (American edition) is published. The film of *The Collector* is released by Columbia Pictures Corp.
1966	*The Magus* (British edition) is published.
1968	A revised edition of *The Aristos* appears. The

film of *The Magus* is released by Twentieth-Century Fox Film Corp.

1969   *The French Lieutenant's Woman* is published. Fowles wins the Silver Pen Award from the English Center of the International P.E.N. (International Association of Poets, Playwrights, Editors, Essayists, and Novelists) for *The French Lieutenant's Woman*.

1970   Fowles is awarded the W. H. Smith and Son Literary Award for *The French Lieutenant's Woman*.

1973   *Poems* is published.

1974   *The Ebony Tower* is published. Fowles writes the text for a book of photographs entitled *Shipwreck*.

1977   A revised edition of *The Magus* appears in Britain. *Daniel Martin* is published. Fowles's translation (with introduction) of Claire de Durfort's *Ourika* is privately published by Thomas Taylor, Austin, Texas.

1978   The revision of *The Magus* appears in the United States.

1

Introduction

I am a writer; I want no more specific prison
than that I express myself in printed words.
—Preface to the revised edition of *The Aristos*.[1]

Even if the pleasure of writing surpasses all other
pleasures for the writer, as it seems to do for John
Fowles, there comes a time when writing alone is
simply not enough. One must also publish and culti-
vate an audience. Considering the vast number of
books published each year and the competition from
the other media for the all too limited attention of
today's reading public, how is the serious writer to
make his mark? How is his work to impress us with
sufficient force to be remembered and preserved?

John Fowles has addressed himself to these questions in an essay entitled "My Recollections of Kafka,"
claiming that the fiction of Franz Kafka provides one
clear model for success.[2] Kafka's work remains with us
so vividly, says Fowles, because he has so severely
limited his field and his method. That is to say, he has
repeatedly described the same or similar experiences
in a similar style. Kafka's, however, is not the only
way, and Fowles has quite consciously chosen a different path. "My obsession," he admits in the same article,
"is with new (to myself) writing worlds, not the con-
solidation of one chosen old one."

Fowles's fantasy—he is reported to have called it once, no doubt with tongue in cheek, his "ambition"—is "to write one book in every imaginable genre."[3] Although he did not begin writing until he was well into his twenties and was not published until he was almost forty, he seems as likely a candidate as any serious writer today to approach that end. He has already showed himself adventurous enough to experiment with a great diversity of styles and subject matter, and confident enough to publish in a wide variety of genres, including different novel forms, short stories, poems, filmscripts, a book of personal philosophy, translations from French, literary criticism, popular journalism, and an assortment of other nonfiction and occasional pieces. He has yet to attempt to write for the theater, although his first-published novel, *The Collector*, has had at least two dramatic renditions.[4]

All of this has been accomplished in a publishing career of only a decade and a half. Apparently, there are as many unpublished manuscripts in his possession as there are published ones. Fowles's interests are wide-ranging, his erudition considerable. He is proud of being a generalist in an age of narrow specialization. One is struck by the sheer ambition of the man, the hugeness of his vision, and the energy and brilliance of its realization.

"If I were to specify my aims in life," he said in an early interview, "I'd first of all like to be a good poet, then a sound philosopher, then a good novelist. The novel is simply, for me, a way of expressing my view of life."[5] Although he has published a book of poems and another (*The Aristos*) concerned with his personal philosophy of life and art, Fowles is neither a good poet nor a philosopher, and to this he now readily admits. His great gift for narrative, however, is undeniable, as is the intellectual and erotic appeal of his fiction, which often titillates and educates simultaneously.

It is, then, as a novelist that Fowles has so clearly made his mark, and it is primarily as a novelist that he will be treated in this book. Each of the following chapters is devoted to a separate work of fiction; this one more generally to the man: his life, his work, and his thought. While Fowles projects the image of himself as a private and reclusive man, he seems not at all reticent about discussing his work and his past. He has granted interviews from the very beginning of his publishing career, and has spoken or written quite often and with candor of his life and his interests.

He was born on the last day of March, 1926, in Leigh-on-Sea, Essex, a small suburban town at the mouth of the Thames. According to his own retrospective account, the town was dominated by the conformist pursuit of respectability: "The rows of respectable little houses inhabited by respectable little people had an early depressive effect on me, and I believe that they partly caused my intense and continuing dislike of mankind *en masse*."[6] Fowles today is a staunch individualist, avoiding as well as one can the tremendous pressures to conform operating in our mass society. "People need more than food," he says in *The Aristos*, "and all the other things they need flourish best when the crowd is least; that is, peace, education, space, and individuality."[7] He is consistently drawn to eccentrics and dissenters past or present, who have had the courage, imagination, and moral conviction to live wholly and uniquely a life of their own.[8] This is also the life style promoted in his fiction. The individual struggling to maintain his individuality, struggling to achieve a measure of self-realization amidst the undirected or misdirected masses, is an important unifying theme throughout his entire corpus.

Fowles passed his early years in Essex. For a while, during World War II, however, his family was evacuated to escape the Luftwaffe's night raids over the area. The youth of fifteen now found himself in a small Devonshire village just south of Dartmoor, one of the least spoiled countrysides remaining in the southwest of England. Here, in vivid contrast to the tame and respectable suburbia he knew in Essex, Fowles received his initiation into the beauty and mystery of nature. This "Huck Finn existence," as he was later to term it,[9] provided another major formative experience in his life. In fact, Fowles now claims to need the company of nature more than the company of people. For him, it is therapeutic. He is, to this day, a knowledgeable and passionate naturalist, natural history having become the dominant outside interest of his adult life.

Fowles is also keenly aware that the other profound influence on his youth was the Bedford School, a typical elite boarding school at which he received his formal education from the ages of fourteen to eighteen. Unable to cope with the social and academic pressures, in combination with the regular brutalities of English boarding school life, the lad suffered "a sort of nervous breakdown."[10] Fortunately for him, it was at this time that his family was evacuated to Devonshire. After a term away, Fowles apparently recovered completely, returned to the Bedford School, and proved an excellent scholar and athlete. He seems at this point to have embraced the system wholeheartedly. He devoted much of his school life to cricket and also rose to the position of "head boy," or chief prefect. As principal disciplinarian over hundreds of younger boys, Fowles came to understand very well and experience intensely the ruthless exercise of power, the manipulation of the law, and the whole system of reward and punishment, conformity and dissent. "Ever since," he recalls, "I have had a violent hatred of leaders, organizers, bosses: of anyone who thinks it good to get or have arbitrary power over other people."[11]

It is not at all surprising, therefore, that the use and abuse of power plays so prominent a part in Fowles's thought. Beginning with *The Collector,* each of his published novels and stories is deeply concerned with the power and control that some people can have over others. "Existence," he says in *The Aristos,* "is the ability to emit power and be affected by power. Power eats or is eaten. To be alive is power."[12]

After leaving the Bedford School, Fowles spent a term at the University of Edinburgh as part of his two-year compulsory military service as a lieutenant in the Royal Marines. His military training, however, finished the day the war ended, and he never experienced combat duty. It was also at this time that Fowles finally gave up hunting. As a youth he was an avid butterfly collector and game hunter. "I've completely rejected that now," he says. "I loathe guns and people who collect living things."[13] By the time he finished his service in the marines, he also seems to have ended his complicity with the British bourgeoisie. Instead of joining the establishment, he, like so many other sensitive young people of his generation and the next, found it necessary to revolt consciously against his middle-class background.

Following his military service, Fowles returned to the university, this time to New College, Oxford, where he received his B.A. (Honors) in 1950. He studied French language and literature, and came strongly under the influence of the post-war existentialist writers, who, no doubt, provided him with a ready-made image for his revolt. He gradually transformed their philosophy and lifestyle into something very personal and very much his own. Today he still retains a distinct sympathy for the moralistic aspect of existentialist philosophy.

Upon leaving Oxford, he taught English at the University of Poitiers, then at a boys school on the island of Spetsai, Greece (the prototype of the island school in *The Magus*). His feeling for Greece—for the independent life of the peasants, the landscape and pine forests, the sea, the special light of the sun, the felt silence—is recorded in *The Magus* and in the "Greek Poems" in the collection entitled *Poems*. As he says in the poem "A Kind of Philhellene," Greece is still the place where one must confront the basic existential questions:

> Who art thou?
> Where from?
> Where to?
> And for thy bread, what dost thou do?

Greece, France, and, of course, England—the country of his birth and the country he has chosen to call home—are the three lands in which Fowles recognizes his roots: "A great deal of what I like in humanity—especially the fight to maintain a freedom of the individual—resides in that triangle of cultures. I feel much more European than British."[14]

Both Fowles's thought and his writing bear witness to his cosmopolitanism. While many of his contemporaries in England, the United States, and Canada seem still to aim at a provincial audience, Fowles has always assumed an international one. He claims to live without nationalistic feeling and entirely apart from the London literary establishment. "Various things," he writes,

have long made me feel an exile in England. Some years ago I came across a sentence in an obscure French novel [Claire de Durfort's *Ourika*, 1824]: *Ideas are the only motherland.* Ever since I have kept it as the most succinct summary I know of what I believe."[15]

The artist figures in his fiction, or those with insight and imagination, also live apart from their fellows in self-appointed exile, and represent a testimony to his contempt for narrow-minded provincialism.

He married Elizabeth Whitton in 1956, and continued to support himself and his wife by assuming various teaching and administrative posts in educational institutions in and around London. It was only with the publication of *The Collector* in 1963 and the sale of the film rights that Fowles could finally afford to be a full-time writer. Relieved of the burden of having to teach for a living, he has been able to live the solitary, routineless existence he prefers to all others.

He and his wife now spend most of the year in Lyme Regis, Dorset (the setting of the first half of *The French Lieutenant's Woman*). They live in a large, comfortable house built in 1780, a few minutes' walk to the sea in one direction and to the woods in another. Though somewhat of a curiosity to the townsfolk, Fowles is generally not bothered by callers or acquaintances and can go about his business unhampered and unobserved. His "business" out of doors is largely a matter of observing the diverse topography of the place and its rich flora and fauna. He also spends a good deal of time in his garden. Unlike the typical English garden, it covers about two acres, is largely wild, and represents Fowles's experiment in conservation and natural living. He has trained himself to look at familiar and ordinary natural life as if it were neither familiar nor ordinary. The smallest details of his garden are observed with continual pleasure and wonder, bringing a sense of harmonious creation into his daily life.

In addition to gardening, walking by the sea or in the woods, and observing birds and insects, Fowles is drawn to other solitary or private activities. He enjoys browsing through book shops and antique stores (he has a penchant for forgotten books and prints, as well as an eye for antique china), reading and listening to music at home, and film-going (especially in London where he always spends some time each year). The portrait is of a person who is equally able to find pleasure and solace in the worlds of nature or the imagination as in the world with other people.

Fowles's imagination, as glimpsed through his fiction and occasional remarks, is densely associative and highly erotic. He tends to view himself in terms of his imaginative life, and his prose fiction he sees as the embodiment of it. He surely feels most alive while in the process of creating: "My real self is here and now, writing. Whenever I think of this . . . experience, images to do with exploring, singlehanded voyages, lone mountain ascents always spring unwanted to my mind."[16]

Fowles has no writing routine and can go for long periods of time without writing anything. When the inspiration comes upon him, however, he can work sixteen hours a day and write with unusual speed, producing sometimes as many as 10,000 words a day. The first drafts of *The Collector* and *The Ebony Tower* were written in less than a month. "You have to do it in a gush, conceive in passion," he says. "You bring up the child later, by reason and logic."[17]

Invention of character, situation, even dialogue seem to come very easily to Fowles. He says that his mind "is constantly wandering off. . . . If they ever want to evolve a way of picking out the prospective novelists among children, this should be the aspect to go for, this drifting off."[18] He generally enjoys the rich profusion and eroticism of his fantasy life. In fact, some of the initial creative process seems to occur in the state between his sleeping and waking, when images float uncontrollably through his mind.

The best exposition of this process can be found in Fowles's own account of the genesis of *The French Lieutenant's Woman*. It begins with the specific figure associated with that novel, but then expands to reveal the creative process and Fowles's writing habits more generally, and so has been quoted at length.

It started . . . as a visual image. A woman stands at the end of a deserted quay and stares out to sea. That was all. This image rose in my mind one morning when I was still in bed half asleep. It corresponded to no actual incident in my life (or in art) that I can recall, though I have for many years collected obscure books and forgotten prints, all sorts of flotsam and jetsam from the last two or three centuries, relics of past lives—and I suppose this leaves me with a sort of dense hinterland from which such images percolate down to the coast of consciousness.

These mythopoeic "stills" (they seem almost always static) float into my mind very often. I ignore them, since that is the best way of finding whether they really are the door into a new world.

So I ignored this image; but it recurred. Imperceptibly it stopped coming to me. I began deliberately to recall it and to try to analyze and hypothesize why it held some sort of imminent power. It was obviously mysterious. . . . I began to fall in love with her. Or with her stance. I didn't know which.

This—not literally—pregnant female image came at a time . . . when I was already halfway through another novel and had, still have, three or four others planned to follow it. It was an interference, but of such power that it soon came to make the previously planned work seem the intrusive element in my life. This accidentality of inspiration has to be allowed for in writing, both in the work one is on (unplanned development of character, unintended incidents, and so on) and in one's works as a whole. Follow the accident, fear the fixed plan—that is the rule.[19]

While writing the rough draft of a novel, Fowles is principally attentive to the flow of the story-line and the overall narrative technique. After its completion, he will often shelve a manuscript for many months, sometimes indefinitely. The first draft of *The Magus*, for instance, was written more than a decade before the novel was published. *The Collector*, albeit the first work he sent to his publisher, was actually his eighth or ninth manuscript. He is, then, usually at work on more than one book at a time.

This fact may help to account for the remarkable consistency of thought and the regular occurrence of certain fundamental concepts from one book to the next. Also, of course, Fowles was thirty-seven years of age and a mature thinker by the time his first book was published. He was a man with breadth and depth of experience. He was (and still is) a habitual and omnivorous reader of considerable erudition, with certain central thoughts and moral convictions around which might crystallize a personal philosophy of life and art.

Still, considering the stylistic variety of his corpus, it is surprising that the work should be so consistent in terms of the thought. Regardless of the time, place, or action of his plots, the essential human situations and problems described remain quite similar, as do the philosophical questions raised and the moral judgments stated or implied. The recurrence of the same or similar ideas in his essays and even in the most recently published *Daniel Martin*, however, unfortunately give the impression of redundancy as well as consistency. He seems preoccupied—obsessed is an equally apt description—with certain ideas and situations to which he returns again and again.

Fowles is a moralist. He has very strong likes and especially dislikes, and tends to express these plainly and forcefully. His works possess obvious moral or didactic elements. In an interview at the outset of his publishing career, Fowles had already confessed: "I feel I must be committed, that I must use literature as a method of propagating my view of life." Again, there appears in the same interview another key statement characterizing his work: "I think the serious writer has to have his view of the purpose of literature absolutely clear. I don't see that you can write seriously without having a philosophy of both life and literature to back you."[20] The main text for that philosophy is *The Aristos*, the original sub-title of which is "a self-portrait in ideas."

When asked if there were a particular picture of the world that he wanted to develop in his work, Fowles responded:

Freedom, yes. How you achieve freedom. That obsesses me. All my books are about that. The question is, is there really free-will? Can we choose freely? Can we act freely? Can we *choose*? How do we do it?[21]

The Aristos makes it clear that Fowles dismisses simplistic answers to these questions. He realizes that freedom of will is not absolute, that it is relative to the freedom allowed by the biological, social, and environmental conditions of each of us. A greater measure of "relative freedom," however, may be brought about by true social equality and by higher and better standards of education.

While *The Aristos* presents the issues, the novels are predicated on the supposition of individual free will and the ideal of self-realization. Their conceptual focus remains on the nature and limits of human freedom, the power and responsibility that freedom entails, and the cruelty and necessity of conscious choice. The

conditions of freedom and self-knowledge are everywhere conjoined in Fowles's work. Self-knowledge is
the goal of life experience and formal education. It is
the end toward which all of his protagonists grope.

Human freedom and the existence of a god who
intervenes in the affairs of men are, for Fowles, mutu-
ally exclusive conditions. "If there had been a creator,"
he quips in *The Aristos,* "his second act would have
been to disappear,"[22] thus allowing us to shape our
identities for ourselves.

The freedom to choose and to change must be ex-
ercised and the full responsibility for ourselves must
be accepted. This, however, is only half of the mature
human condition. The other half recognizes just as
plainly the tremendous force of all that has brought us
to the present moment, and the power of the past to
keep us moving in the same direction. To choose to
change is no easy task. Accordingly, Fowles's fiction
tends to focus upon those crucial moments when important choices are made and when they are set in
motion by ensuing actions. The fiction stresses the
existential shock so often necessary to jolt us into a
full awareness of the moment of choice and the need
to act upon this awareness. Freedom is generally explored along two paths simultaneously: the ethical or
moral path, by involving us in the quest of the fictional
characters; and the aesthetic, by illuminating the
liberating possibilities, for reader and writer alike, of
fiction itself.

Creating a work of art, for Fowles, is the supreme
expression of the freedom to be who you are: "Being
an artist is first discovering the self and then stating
the self in self-chosen terms."[23] In addition to its basic
functions of teaching and amusing, Fowles believes
that art also has the unorthodox function of stimulat-
ing insecurity, of making us aware of the rule of hazard in our lives. "What good science tries to eliminate,"

he writes, "good art seeks to provoke—mystery, which is lethal to the one, and vital to the other."[24]

Although Fowles equivocates in his use of the term, the central meaning of "mystery" in his work, and surely its meaning above, is the antithesis of that which is known or knowable. It is conceived as man's source of energy, the dynamic spur to human achievement, because the very fact of mystery allows for the continued existential quest. To live with it and to harness, not eliminate, the dynamic power of such a life is the ultimate goal. Fowles's fiction assumes a function almost religious in nature when it is able to evoke the unknown and to involve the reader relationally with it. These moments provide us with experiences akin to what is traditionally associated with the realm of the holy or sacred. The concept, however, need not be confined to the sphere of religion. Fowles's "mystery," for example, functions similarly to what John Keats called "negative capability," that is, the distinguishing mark of the great poet, who is "capable of being in uncertainties, mysteries, doubts without any irritable reaching after fact and reason."[25]

The fundamental fact of existence, for Fowles, is the tension or conflict of opposites: "We all live at the crossroad of myriad irreconcilable poles, or opposing factions. Their irreconcilability constitutes our cell, and the discovery of living with and utilizing this irreconcilability constitutes our escape."[26] These "irreconcilable poles," such as knowledge and mystery, security and insecurity, or comfort and pain, are recognized and defined in terms of each other. They tug on the self in opposite directions. These unresolved tensions, however, are a blessing to humanity for they promote and foster the basic activities of living.

Love and sexuality play a crucial role in causing and relieving the tensions of human existence. Perhaps for this reason, Fowles, in his writing, is engaged in the exploration and exposition of the nature of love and the criteria for harmonious relations between the sexes. Some of the fundamental problems of society, he contends, arise from our confusion of "the drive towards sexual experience (in itself part of a deeper drive towards the hazardous and adventurous) and the drive towards love as institutionalized in marriage (in itself part of the drive towards certainty and security)."[27]

Heterosexual love and the nature of freedom are at the thematic center of all of Fowles's work. In fact, in the novels, the two are inextricably bound: the realization of love brings with it a sense of freedom, and the responsible assumption of one's freedom allows for the full realization of the possibilities of love. The erotic quality of the fiction is but one aspect of the broader concern. Fowles was an avowed feminist before it was fashionable to be so, and some of his non-fiction pieces illustrate with equal clarity his concern for the harmonious relations between the sexes.[28] A study of the permutations on the basic themes will help us to compare the various novels and to view the corpus as a unified whole.

2

The Collector

Having, not being, governs our time.—*The Aristos*[1]

John Fowles had been writing fiction for a decade before he offered *The Collector* to the public in 1963. In fact, *The Magus* (published in 1965) and other as yet unpublished novels were already in rough draft before he wrote *The Collector*. It is less surprising to us who know this than to his reviewers that his first-published novel should contain so few indications of the novice. While *The Collector* is less elaborate than the other novels in terms of its structure and more modest in terms of its plot and themes, it is perhaps Fowles's most finely wrought and carefully organized long piece of fiction.

The plot is highly compressed, uncomplicated by the subplots and digressions that characterize his other novels. It is the very carefully controlled, often horrifying account of a lepidopterist who turns his attention from rare butterflies to young and beautiful women. Fowles says that he came upon the idea for the novel first from viewing a performance of Bartok's opera, *Bluebeard's Castle,* in which he was particularly impressed by the symbolism of the man imprisoning women underground; and then, about a year later, from an actual incident reported in the newspapers of a London boy who captured a girl and imprisoned her

in an air-raid shelter for over three months before her
eventual rescue.[2] Fowles altered the ending of this
story, endowed the broad outline of events with
credible details, painted imaginative psychological
portraits, and made of the whole a significant contemporary social commentary.

The "collector" is one Frederick (though he prefers to call himself Ferdinand) Clegg, the twenty-five-
year-old orphaned son of lower-middle-class parents.
He lives a stifled existence with his ignorant, pietistic
Aunt Annie and his crippled cousin Mabel, and he
holds an unimportant job as a clerk in a town-hall
office near London. Clegg suffers from an acute sense
of class inferiority and personal inadequacy, coupled
with a fear of failure and criticism. This self-conscious
and small-minded, friendless and graceless young man
has little prospect for personal development or fulfill-
ment of any kind until the day he strikes it rich in the
football pools, which he has been playing weekly during the previous five years. The check he receives is for
"£73,091 and some odd shillings and pence," the
equivalent in the early 1960s of more than $200,000.
It is his sudden wealth that incites Clegg to turn his
secret, psychopathic fantasy into a concrete reality,
and it is his plans and their eventualities that form
the basis for the plot of the novel.

The object of his fantasy is the beautiful art student, Miranda Grey. She is everything he is not:
imaginative, open-minded, gifted, liberal, humane.
She possesses a vitality and a capacity for love and
sympathy that are quite incomprehensible to the petty
clerk. While she, in her own way, is also smug and
priggish, it is clear that Miranda is to be seen as the
flawed but certainly more positive product of the
upper-middle class, with the sadly unrealized potential to become, as Fowles himself says, "the kind of
being humanity so desperately needs."[3] These two

characters, then, embody individual and social polari-
ties, and it is largely through the clash of their personalities and perspectives that the meaning of the novel
emerges.

When the novel opens, we are to understand that
Frederick has for some time been an admirer of the
lovely Miranda, though always surreptitiously and
from a distance. He derives vicarious satisfaction from
his daydreams about what their lives together might
be. The scenario for his adolescent and narcissistic
fantasy strikes the reader at once as pathetic yet ludi-
crous in its gross, cliché-ridden oversimplification of
bourgeois life and love:

She drew pictures and I looked after my collection (in my
dreams). It was always she loving me and my collection,
drawing and coloring them; working together in a beautiful
modern house in a big room with one of those huge glass
windows; meetings there of the Bug Section, where instead
of saying almost nothing in case I made mistakes we were
the popular host and hostess. She all pretty with her pale
blonde hair and grey eyes and of course the other men all
green round the gills.

The voyeur observes her as he would a butterfly,
reducing her free and vital nature in his mind's eye
to the status of an object, a "specimen" in a collection.
This life-destroying power of the collector, this objectification of another human being, is manifest from the
beginning in the language of Clegg's narrative. When
he sees her, for example, he notes the fact in his "ento-
mological observations diary" ("at first with X, and
then when I knew her name with M"); he compares
her hair to "Burnet cocoons" and spying on her to the
experience of "catching a rarity . . . a Pale Clouded
Yellow, for instance." Later Miranda identifies herself
with the butterfly "he has always wanted to catch,"
desperately "fluttering against the glass" of the "killing

bottle." The imagery of stalking, capturing, chloro-forming, mounting, and exhibiting is sustained through-out the novel. The details of butterfly collecting are rendered accurately, perhaps from Fowles's first-hand knowledge of the hobby as a boy.

Clegg's new-found wealth and the awkward and tasteless expenditures that follow its acquisition do nothing for his ego: "They still treated me behind the scenes for what I was—a clerk. It was no good throw-ing money around. As soon as we spoke or did some-thing we gave the game away." He has, however, all the money he needs to ship off his aunt and cousin to Australia for an extended visit with relatives, thus freeing him for the indulgence of his growing interest in pornography and his fantasies of Miranda, which at this point he insists upon trying to keep quite dis-tinct. His absorption in Miranda seems ironically and rather pathetically to raise his self-esteem:

I read in the paper the other day (Saying of the Day)— "What Water is to the Body, Purpose is to the Mind." That is very true, in my humble opinion. When Miranda became the purpose of my life I should say I was at least as good as the next man, as it turned out.

Clegg purchases in Sussex an old, secluded cot-tage with a secret cellar, renovates and decorates the place, and outfits it with clothes, books, and other things he imagines will please Miranda. With dia-bolical precision he secures the place against her escape. One night, while she is returning from the cinema, he entices her to his van, chloroforms her, and abducts her to his new home, where she is to remain indefinitely as his "guest." The cold, dank basement, lacking fresh air and sunlight, with "walls like wet wood in winter," provides an intolerable environment for Miranda. Denying her access to radio, television, and newspapers, Frederick hopes that she will soon

grow accustomed to her new surroundings, turn her
thoughts to him, and even grow to "love" him. Most
of the ensuing action is confined to this alien, claustrophobic environment, the physical counterpart to the
mind and soul of its designer.

The remainder of the story deals with the intimate but perverse relationship that develops between
the collector and his specimen, with Frederick's de-
mented efforts to satisfy her needs and Miranda's
repeated attempts to secure her release. The reader is
at once repelled and fascinated by this apparently fantastic series of events. It seems perfectly plausible,
however, because it is presented realistically and in
minute detail. Though titillating throughout, the material is always handled with decorum and control. It
is greatly to his credit that Fowles never allows the
novel to descend to the level of sadism or sensational-
ism on the one hand, nor to sentimentality on the
other.

At first Miranda guesses that the motive is sex,
but, after her awkward and unsuccessful attempt at
seduction, she discovers what the reader has known
from the beginning, that Clegg is not only imagina-
tively impotent but sexually impotent as well. All her
efforts to penetrate and alter the mentality of the
collector, to communicate her own rudimentary emotional needs, to woo him and win him over, end in
dismal failure. Despite their physical proximity, there
is no bridge to span the separation between them.
After wooing and seducing; after bargaining, begging,
pleading, and play acting; after desperately trying
every possible means of escape, including an attempt
to burrow out and even an attack on his person with
an axe, Miranda contracts pneumonia in the dank
basement. Her incarceration ends implacably with a
lonely, frightening, miserable death.

"Well," says Clegg, "I shut her mouth up and got

the eyelids down. I didn't know what to do then, I
went and made myself a cup of tea." He briefly fantasizes suicide and a common burial, "like Romeo and
Juliet," a "real tragedy," which he believes could
finally bring him "some proper respect." He quickly
abandons this idea, and the novel ends with Clegg
contemplating the problems of maintaining another
"guest"—this time one with more modest aspirations,
a shopgirl from Woolworth's.

The open-ended conclusion, first evidenced in *The
Collector*, is a characteristic feature of Fowles's fiction.
Here it suggests that the collector is bound to the
cyclical enactment of his psychopathic fantasies. In
Fowles's later novels the open-ended conclusions will
suggest fresh beginnings and hitherto unthought-of
potentialities in the lives of the protagonists.

The story, then, is quite simple. All but the final
details are related in the first part, that is, the first
120 pages, of the novel. Its subtlety and its extraordinary portraiture, however, arise almost entirely from
the complexity of the narrative technique. Fowles
allows his antagonists to tell their own stories, thus
achieving a double perspective on the otherwise
straightforward sequence of events. Each of them provides his own rendition, Frederick's first-person narrative framing Miranda's, which takes the form of a
diary kept secretly during her captivity and discovered
by her captor after her death. (The use of Clegg's
story to frame Miranda's was an afterthought and
came as a recommendation from Fowles's editor. The
author had originally submitted the two accounts in
sequence, thereby neglecting the element of suspense
arising from delaying the presentation of the details
of the final moments.[4]) From the conflation of these
partial, subjective accounts, the reader gains a more
objective and inclusive perspective on the events and

their meaning, and a much fuller, more sophisticated understanding of the motives of the title character.

Clegg, of course, is allowed to condemn himself even before Miranda fills in the details from her point of view. His banal confession reveals much more clearly than Clegg himself ever realizes just how repressive his upbringing has been and how warped are his values. Indeed, much of the irony of his story arises from the fact that he unwittingly reveals more than he understands. Much of its horror arises from the apparently clinical, matter-of-fact manner in which he recounts his fiendish plot. A considerable part of his narrative is devoted to rationalizing or justifying his actions, and especially to denying his culpability, until we come to realize that Clegg does not fully understand what he is doing and therefore is not fully accountable for his actions. He frequently suggests that the plot was unpremeditated, that the events occurred by chance not by choice. About purchasing the cottage, for example, he claims: "I didn't go down there with the intention of seeing whether there was anywhere to have a secret guest. I can't really say what intention I had." Concerning the elaborate preparations for his "guest," he says:

All this time I never thought it was serious. . . . I used to say, of course, I'll never do it, this is only pretending. And I wouldn't have pretended even like that if I hadn't had all the time and money I wanted. In my opinion a lot of people who may seem happy now would do what I did or similar things if they had the money and the time. I mean, to give way to what they pretend now they shouldn't. Power corrupts, a teacher I had always said. And money is power.

Miranda's death, Clegg twice claims, "came unexpectedly," and "it was not my fault. How was I to know she was iller than she looked."

In spite of everything Clegg does and says, it is remarkable that his tale still manages to evoke some sympathy in us, as we gain insight into the private hell in which he suffers. He is fundamentally not responsible for his actions. The possessor is himself possessed; he is as much the victim as the victimizer. After the seduction scene, for instance, he expresses his self-conscious agony, his sex shame, in the following candid confession:

I was like mad when I got out. I can't explain. I didn't sleep the whole night. It kept on coming back, me standing and lying there with no clothes on, the way I acted and what she must think. I could just see her laughing at me down there. Every time I thought about it, it was like my whole body went red. I didn't want the night to end. I wanted it to stay dark forever.

When we turn from Clegg's narrative to Miranda's diary, comprising Part Two of *The Collector*, we are immediately aware of a radical departure in perspective and style. The events beginning with her capture and ending with her loss of consciousness are retold from her point of view, with, of course, changes of emphasis, deletions and additions, as well as long passages about her past life, her goals, and her social and aesthetic values. The first entry, on the seventh night of her captivity, describes what Clegg could only dimly grasp and what we could hitherto only imagine: the terror of the "crypt room," the anxiety arising from the uncertainty of her situation, the "terrible" silence. She rightly identifies power as the major force governing their relationship. And yet, typical of Miranda's complex and ambivalent viewpoint, she still must admit: "A strange thing. He fascinates me."

One of the most interesting aspects of the diary is the way it records Miranda's coming to terms with her situation, trying to make sense of its evident absurdity and trying to understand the motives of her captor. It is the testimony of her repeated efforts to sympathize with Clegg and to educate him, of her refusal to relinquish hope, to admit that humaneness, sympathy, and intelligence count for nothing in the crypt room. The insight she provides into their growing intimacy is especially noteworthy: the feeling she has of their "linked destiny"; the scorn and compassion she feels for his miserable life and the lives of his aunt and cousin, the "great dull hopeless weight of it"; her sensitivity to "his sex neurosis and his class neurosis and his uselessness and his emptiness."

Part Two is far from the clinical, uncritical, unimaginative matter-of-factness characteristic of so much of Part One. Instead of the unwitting irony in Clegg's account, we are treated to Miranda's conscious irony and even an occasional display of humor—this despite everything that has happened to her. In the second week of her incarceration, for example, appears the following note:

Incident. Today at lunch I wanted the Worcester sauce. He hardly ever forgets to bring anything I might want. But no Worcester sauce. So he gets up, goes out, undoes the padlock holding the door open, locks the door, gets the sauce in the outer cellar, unlocks the door, re-padlocks it, comes back. And then looks surprised when I laugh.

The basis for the perception of humor here lies in the disparity between the energy exerted and the importance of the task, a perception that entirely escapes the monomaniacal Clegg. We are used to laughing at overly fastidious, obsessive, or purely mechanical behavior in comedy, but *The Collector* is in no way a comedy and its humor (the little that there is) is far from pure. Rather than providing "comic relief" from the situation, the humorous moments of the novel, more often than not, augment the feelings of anxiety

and menace. In this respect *The Collector* is aligned
with the work of Fowles's theatrical contemporaries,
the contributors to the so-called theater of the absurd,
represented by Harold Pinter, Samuel Beckett, and
Eugene Ionesco among others, whose plays also are
frequently restricted to an imprisoning one-room setting. That Clegg is devoid of a sense of humor, that
he is as unable to grasp the incongruities inherent in
their situation as he is to discover the imaginative
possibilities outside of it, is further indication to
Miranda and to us of his pathological imbalance.

Because of the conventional assumption in the
diary form that the writer is the only reader (or, as
Miranda says, that she is "talking to herself"), we
must assume that we are getting a very private glimpse
into the innermost thoughts and feelings of the diarist.
We are thus ironically required to imagine ourselves
in an analogous role to Clegg's, the role of the voyeur,
reading what was never intended for us to read, and
gaining vicarious enjoyment from this experience.

Miranda keeps her diary as a means of maintaining her sanity, as an imaginative and intellectual
retreat—"to escape," as she says, "in spirit if not in
fact." Naturally enough, she devotes much of her time
to nostalgic reminiscence of the joy and excitement
of life outside her prison, and especially of the influence of one particular artist friend, "G.P." (George
Paston). He was Miranda's first and only mentor, and
the pages of her diary reveal his influence on her
intellectual, emotional, and aesthetic development, a
development cut pathetically short. The sections recalling G.P.'s thought and life style contain embryonic
expressions of Fowles's own philosophy, which receives
much fuller treatment in the expository prose of *The
Aristos* and the remarkable reflections in *The Magus*
and *The French Lieutenant's Woman.* Too often in the
passages of *The Collector,* however, the reader senses

that Miranda has stepped out of character and is serving mainly and too obviously as her author's mouthpiece. Despite this stylistic flaw, these overtly didactic passages do make a primary contribution to the development of the themes of the novel.

Miranda depicts herself (perhaps a little too melodramatically) as a martyred representative of "the few" and Clegg as the embodiment of what she calls "the Calibans" and what G.P. calls "the New People." Each of these two terms is associated with a separate pattern of imagery in *The Collector*, one exclusively literary in its reference, the other social. The first, "the Calibans," involves an elaborate analogy between *The Collector* and Shakespeare's *The Tempest*. Miranda, who goes through the entire experience believing that Clegg's given name is Ferdinand, articulates the ironic correspondence between their relationship and that of the young romantic lovers of the same names who are united in matrimonial bliss at the conclusion of Shakespeare's play. While this ending remains only an unfulfilled wish for Clegg, the two "Ferdinands" seem in a similar situation and seem motivated by a similar impulse: "Might I but through my prison once a day/ Behold this maid." In these terms, Frederick may be said to burlesque the noble character of Ferdinand, while Miranda fails miserably even to simulate his romantic ideal.

The inverted analogy with Shakespeare's romance is maintained throughout *The Collector* by a stroke of genius: Fowles has Miranda re-christen, and thus more accurately characterize, her tormentor as Caliban, the half-human offspring of the witch Sycorax, who unsuccessfully attempts to rape the innocent Miranda. The brute is subdued and the maiden is saved by the dominant figure of Shakespeare's play, Miranda's father-magician, Prospero. The magician figure, who can harness the positive forces of the universe and control the beastly and violent impulses of men, is conspicuously absent from *The Collector* (unless G.P. is interpreted as playing this role in Miranda's psyche, in which case he is ultimately impotent in the confrontation with Caliban). The magician figure assumes a prominent position in *The Magus*, in which it is not fortuitous that allusions to *The Tempest* reappear.

The other image pattern, with its social implications, is associated with G.P.'s coinage "the New People." According to this line of interpretation, the struggle between Frederick and Miranda is an allegory (Fowles himself uses the term "parable"[5]). The characters' situation represents the omnipresent struggle between two much greater opponents: the faithless and visionless, the materialist and philistine masses on the one hand, and the few imaginative individuals who create and maintain the best of our civilization on the other. Furthermore, the story of Frederick and Miranda stresses the mindless oppression and ultimate destruction of the physically weak but gifted few by, in Miranda's words, those possessed of the "great deadweight of pettiness and selfishness and meanness."

This conflict between the Few and the Many (as it is called in *The Aristos*) is at least as much an admonition for the future as it is a depiction of the present. Both Frederick and Miranda are products of their very different environments, their vastly unequal educations and opportunities. In the preface to the second edition of *The Aristos,* Fowles states quite explicitly that it was his intention in *The Collector* to illuminate the invidious consequences of these gross social inequalities so characteristic of Western society. Clegg's tyranny and Miranda's abortive attempts to understand and to educate her oppressor point to the need to create a society in which the Many will be tolerant of the Few and the Few will feel responsible for the education and betterment of the Many. If there is a positive morality that emerges from *The Collector,* it is surely this, an idea which also forms a central thesis of *The Aristos.*

While *The Collector* is to be interpreted in social terms, it ought not to be too narrowly restricted to a matter of British class conflict or even to that between the artist and the philistine. However naturally these interpretations arise from Fowles's realistic evocation of place and period, I think they represent far too limited an approach to the novel. To be sure, the back-drop to the drama of Frederick and Miranda is pro-vided by the British class structure, but the immedi-ate setting, while in the midst of British society, is nevertheless entirely separate from it. Once the abduc-tion occurs, once Miranda is confined to the cellar and isolated from her social world, the external references are of a very limited nature. The battleground is much less localized, the issues far more fundamental. What matter most to Miranda in the crypt room are freedom of movement, fresh air, sunlight, and the like.

The Collector, as its title implies, can also be inter-preted in very general terms. Class conflict is but one manifestation of the disparity between the Few and the Many. They are distinguished not only by the benefits derived from the environment, but by genetic endowments as well. While Frederick is depicted as having almost nothing but new-found wealth and Miranda as having nearly everything (or the potential for nearly everything) but freedom, in actual life the distinctions between the "haves" and "have-nots" is not so clear-cut. All of us find ourselves in both groups at different times and with reference to different quali-ties. On one level, Clegg and Miranda are embodi-ments of social tendencies or psychological types irrespective of class, state, and other such particulari-ties. In terms of socio-political types, these polar figures represent the freedom-loving individuals (the existentialists, as Fowles develops the notion in *The Aristos* and *The Magus*) and the would-be or actual tyrants (the fascists, who provide the real ideological contrast to the existentialists).

In terms of abstract psychological types, Fowles has equally well depicted the distinctive features of what Erich Fromm calls the necrophiliac, the type attracted to all that is unalive, sick, or mechanical. Hating life, his activities are largely destructive. He is boring; he kills liveliness in social intercourse; he seemingly possesses the capacity to transform all that he touches into something dead.[6] This is what Fowles has so concretely and economically embodied in the figure of the Collector, and what Miranda, to her horror and disgust, soon discovers about him:

It's me he wants, my look, my outside; not my emotions or my mind or my soul or even my body. Not anything *human*. He's a collector. That's the great dead thing in him.

Opposed to this is Miranda's own self-characterization (constituting what Fromm calls the biophilic type):

I love honesty and freedom and giving. I love making, I love doing. I love being to the full, I love everything which is not sitting and watching and copying and dead at heart.

Perhaps the most wretched thing about Clegg is that he confuses love with his desire for possession. As he himself admits, though without fully understanding the ramifications:

What she never understood was that with me it was having. Having her was enough. Nothing needed doing. I just wanted to have her, and safe at last.

We can now return—with perhaps a fuller understanding of its significance—to the epigraph from *The Aristos* with which this chapter began: "Having,

not being, governs our time." The fundamental significance of *The Collector* is in its depiction of the
drive for possession as the ubiquitous substitute in
the impotent for their inability to love and in the unimaginative for their inability to create. This theme
holds a central position in the Fowles corpus. It is
further developed in *The Magus* and recurs with
subtle variations in the rest of Fowles's published
fiction as well.

3

The Magus

> He knows the Many are like an audience
> under the spell of a conjuror, seemingly
> unable to do anything but serve as material
> for the conjuror's tricks; and he knows
> that the true destiny of man is to become
> a magician himself.—*The Aristos*[1]

> The noblest relationship is marriage,
> that is, love. Its nobility resides
> in its altruism . . . and in its refusal
> ever to regard the other as a thing,
> an object, a utilizability.—*The Aristos*

The Magus was the author's first full-length manuscript. He wrote the original draft in the early 1950s, but he continued, almost obsessively, to rewrite and revise it over the following twenty-five years, that is, over virtually his entire career as a writer. The drafts were collated and reworked in 1964. The novel was published the year after, perhaps because of the need to exorcise its influence by finally severing himself from it and sending it into the world. Even then, however, Fowles was not satisfied with the product. As soon as he saw the first bound copy, he recently noted, Fowles knew that he had published before it was ready.[2]

In 1969 he was quoted as saying: "I hadn't the

technique. The form is inadequate for the content."[3]
And in 1971 he remarked: "I still think *The Magus*
doesn't really work. In the first draft, it just didn't
work at all; I didn't know what frame, what context
to put it in or what style to adopt."[4] Finally in 1977
Fowles published a revised edition of the novel, representing his line by line revision of the whole. Because, at the time of writing this chapter, the new
edition had not appeared in the United States, I
based this discussion on the first version of the novel,
the one with which most readers will be familiar.
However, because of the rarity of such a publishing
phenomenon and because Fowles's revisions have sub-
stantially altered the original, I have appended to
this chapter an account of the revised edition based on
the British text.

The Magus is the seminal piece in the Fowles
corpus, not so much because it is the first as because
it expresses, with varying degrees of clarity and maturity, the main preoccupations of his *oeuvre*. His
other works hark back to the themes and images that
first took shape in the original draft. It shares its key
terms and concepts with *The Aristos*. If *The Aristos,* as
suggested by its original subtitle, represents Fowles's
"self-portrait in ideas," then *The Magus* may be
viewed as a self-portrait in fiction. Having grown out
of Fowles's Oxford years and his experience in Greece,
and having been thereafter subjected to periodic
scrutiny, *The Magus* may be read autobiographically
—though with great caution. Touching upon its genesis in an interview with Daniel Halpern, Fowles has
stated: "In a way the book was a metaphor of my own
personal experience in Greece. An allegory, if you like.
At least that's how it started."[5]

The Magus, as does *The Collector,* deals alle-
gorically with the struggle between the Few and the

Many. Whereas *The Collector* depicts the imprison-
ment and ultimate destruction of the one by the other,
The Magus relates the process of education and libera-
tion necessary for the Few. The figures of the Magus
and the Collector embody the antitheses of love and
possession, creation and destruction, freedom and
bondage. These conceptual distinctions are reflected
in the novels' broad stylistic differences. As related
in the previous chapter, nearly all of the action of *The
Collector* is set within the claustrophobic confines of a
basement prison. There are only two actors and the
plot is highly compressed and condensed. Contrasted
with this, *The Magus*, comprised of story within story
and metaphor within metaphor, is expansive, discur-
sive, and diffuse. Its variety of settings, profusion of
episodes, and abandonment of surface realism suggest
the attempt to transcend the ordinary limits of thought
and action. It concentrates on the illumination of the
possibilities, not the limitations, of human nature.

The protagonist and narrator of *The Magus* are
one and the same person. However, as his story is told
in retrospect, and as his attitudes towards himself and
the world have been shaped by the experiences he
relates, Nicholas Urfe as narrator establishes from the
beginning an ironic detachment from the person he
was, that is, from the character in his story. Much of
the action of Part I is set in London. The year is 1953—
also the year of the first draft of *The Magus*, begun
when Fowles himself was leaving Greece. The first
chapter contains the self-portrait of a young and cyni-
cal aesthete. After two unsuccessful years in the
national service, Nicholas went to Oxford, where he
"began to discover" that he "was not the person [he]
wanted to be." Along with other "fellow odd men,"
he forms a club called *Les Hommes Revoltés*:

We . . . drank very dry sherry, and (as a protest against those shabby duffle-coated last years of the forties) wore dark gray suits and black ties for our meetings; we argued about essence and existence and called a certain kind of inconsequential behavior existentialist. . . . but we didn't realize that the heroes, or anti-heroes, of the French existentialist novels we read were not supposed to be realistic. We tried to imitate them, mistaking metaphorical descriptions of complex modes of feeling for straightforward prescriptions of behavior.

During his second year at university, his parents are killed in a plane crash. Thus, like Frederick Clegg in the previous novel and the hero and heroine of the next one (*The French Lieutenant's Woman*), Nicholas is alone in the world. Aside from the sheer narrative convenience, the elimination of the parents allows Fowles more easily to present his characters in the same way he views people, that is, as fundamentally isolated. (He himself must have felt something of this at an early age, for he mentioned to me that the English public school system "in a sense makes orphans of boys at the age of fourteen," when they leave home for boarding school.[6]) At the death of his parents, Nicholas says that he felt only "relief," a mistaken sense of "freedom." Nicholas will continue to confuse being unattached with being free.

Nicholas manages to obtain a third-class degree from Oxford and a first-class illusion that he is a poet. Despite the pride of a dozen sexual conquests by the time of graduation, he remains loveless, incapable of real emotional intimacy. The introductory chapter ends with Nicholas's declaration that he needs "a new land, a new race, a new language" and, though he could not have phrased it this way at the time, "a new mystery."

This brief portrait establishes Nicholas's main problems and introduces some of the concepts and metaphors which will reverberate throughout the novel and develop its principal themes. Nicholas is deluded about the kind of person he is, uncertain about what or who he wants to become, and unaware of how to effect a change in himself. He understands little of the nature of love and freedom. For the former he substitutes sex and power; he confuses the latter with irresponsible escape from emotional entanglement. As he is also confused about the relationship of life and art, it is not fortuitous that his adolescent existentialist pose quoted above originates from a misapprehension of the value and function of complex metaphor.[7] His confusion of "metaphorical description" and "prescription," however, is only symptomatic of a deeper disorder, namely, his profound sense of separation from the actual world around him. This alienation, of course, is the primary theme of those French existentialist novels that Nicholas admits he had misinterpreted. Finally, Nicholas's closing statement, concerning his need for a new land and a new mystery, foreshadows the main pattern of events in the novel. The primary structural image of *The Magus* is formed by the journey from England to Greece and back to England, and the new realm of experience uncovered is that of mystery.

Nicholas moves to London and there meets Alison Kelly, a "mixed-up" Australian woman, "a kind of human oxymoron" (a metaphor used again for the French Lieutenant's Woman). Alison is a sexual creature, crude but forthright and honest. She is the first woman in his life who has not fallen for his "solitary heart" routine. "Let's cut corners," she says upon first meeting him. "To hell with literature. You're clever and I'm beautiful. Now let's talk about what we really are." Apparently for the first time, Nicholas finds himself talking freely about the intimate details of his life. This is his first love relationship, but he is so distrustful of the emotional life, so "cerebral and self-absorbed," that he manages to deceive himself into believing that what he feels is mere desire.

Alison's only rival at this point is Greece, Nicholas having "fallen in love with the picture" long before seeing "the reality." He has applied, and been accepted, for the position of assistant master of English at the Lord Byron School, on the island of Phraxos, the "fenced" island, modeled after Spetsai, about eighty miles from Athens and six from the Peloponnesian mainland.[8] The lovers part, Nicholas feeling most characteristically that he has "escaped," that Alison loves him more than he does her, and that he has "in some indefinable way won." This imagery, which points to his interpretation of personal relationships in terms of contest, competition, and game, persists throughout Nicholas's narrative. Much to his benefit, Nicholas is soon to discover that "by constantly slipping away one has slipped away. One exists no more, one is no longer free."

He leaves Alison and London far behind—or so he thinks—and arrives in Greece to find it "supremely beautiful," immediately to fall "head over heels totally and forever in love." The Greek landscape sharpens his senses and enlivens his imagination, enabling him more easily to open up to the adventure soon to befall him. Upon first arriving, Nicholas compares his disorientation to Alice entering Wonderland, a land in which all things seem possible, in which conventional ideas and perceptions are subverted.

Nicholas, however, is still himself. Though in love with the land, he is bored with the society of the village and stifled by the routine of the school. He suddenly awakens to the fact that he is not a poet, and destroys his poems in a grand gesture of self-pity. Two small sores he discovers on his body are diag-

nosed as syphilis, a disease he believes he has contracted in an Athens brothel. The isolation, the loneliness, his feeling of being tainted spiritually as well as
physically, allow his deep-seated self-hatred to emerge
on a more conscious level. Near despair, Nicholas
contemplates suicide: "I had created nothing, I be-
longed to nothingness, to the *néant,* and it seemed to
me that my own death was the only thing left that I
could create." He borrows the gatekeeper's rifle, goes
off alone into the hills, and—like an actor in a melo-
drama playing his curtain scene before an impressed
but invisible audience—Nicholas prepares to end his
life. With the realization that he lacks the will to pull
the trigger, comes a confession which lucidly dis-
tinguishes between moral and aesthetic motivation,
and which marks the first significant stage in the evolution of Nicholas's self-awareness:

All the time I felt I was being watched, that I was not
alone, that I was putting on an act for the benefit of someone, that this action could be done only if it was spontaneous, pure, isolated—and moral. Because more and
more it crept through my mind with the chill spring night
that I was trying to commit not a moral action, but a
fundamentally aesthetic one; to do something that would
end my life sensationally, significantly, consistently. It was
a Mercutio death I was looking for, not a real one. A death
to be remembered, not the true death of a true suicide,
the death obliterate.

He re-evaluates himself and concludes that, although he has been genuinely depressed, he has "also
been, and always would be, intensely false; in existentialist terms, unauthentic." His attempt at suicide, as
well as his pursuit of poetry, are now recognized for
what they were, attempts to escape, to construct a
romantic and narcissistic self-portrait which might
substitute for a life of genuine relationship with

others and responsibility for himself. Recognizing
one's faults, however necessary, is not sufficient for
insuring the ability to alter them, and the first part of
the novel concludes with the expression of Nicholas's
belief in an unalterable "pattern of destiny" that for
him is "down and down, and down." "But then," we
are told in the last sentence of Part I, "the mysteries
began."

Let us pause with the action to explore more fully
the character of the protagonist, the structure of meaning and metaphor so far developed, and the direction
in which we are heading. The feeling Nicholas expresses of "being watched" is an experience that is
repeated and a notion that reverberates throughout the
novel. It suggests his continual need to perform for
others and to be evaluated by others. It points, in the
Sartrean terms of his own account, to his "bad faith,"
that is, to his incapacity to accept responsibility for
the deeds he freely performs. *The Magus* is designed
to indicate that the revulsion Nicholas feels at his
"nothingness," his feeling of divorce between himself
and the world, results from a misguided attitude and
not from a fact of nature, not from the human condition. It is in this respect that *The Magus* departs so
radically from the French existentialist novels to provide a more optimistic approach to daily life.

Nicholas is a representative figure of our age and
of Fowles's generation. His alienation stems from a
misapprehension of human possibilities and it is nur-
tured by cynicism ("the dominant tendency of our
contra-suggestible age"). This cynicism he has so carefully cultivated has the effect of shutting him off from
experience by limiting his vision of himself and the
possibilities for relationship with others. Before his
story is ended, Nicholas will come to know himself
better and to understand the existentialist philosophy

he at this point so pathetically mimics. He will learn that the only pattern of destiny is hazard, that there is, in fact, no destiny other than the one which each of us must try to shape for himself.

There is a shift from the normative, day-to-day experience realistically presented in Part I to a fantastic and bizarre world of invention and charade in Part II. This is a world, like Wonderland, in which, it seems, anything may happen. The "first event" occurs when Nicholas hikes to the other side of the island, to the cape called Bourani, on which the secretive and eccentric Maurice Conchis, the Magus of the title, has built his luxurious villa. On the beach, once again, Nicholas has the sensation that he is not alone, that he is being watched. He discovers an anthology of English verse with the following passage from T. S. Eliot's "Little Gidding" underscored in red ink:

> We shall not cease from exploration
> And the end of all our exploring
> Will be to arrive where we started
> And know the place for the first time.

After reading these lines and others by Auden and Pound, he sleeps for a while, then awakens to find that the book has been retrieved. It was apparently left there for his benefit.

The passage from "Little Gidding" is crucial to an understanding of the significance and function of the three-part geographical structure of *The Magus*. The structure, to begin with, is patterned on that of the traditional quest story, involving a voyage to a distant land, the achievement of a mission or the acquisition of special knowledge, and the return home. The last line of the quotation is repeated at the novel's end, after Nicholas has finally come to understand freedom in terms of return instead of escape. He is back in London and has rediscovered Alison: "She was mysterious, almost a new woman; one had to go back several steps, and start again; *and know the place for the first time.*" As used here, "the place" is a metaphor expressing the relationship between Nicholas and Alison, a relationship he ultimately recognizes as love. Nicholas undergoes a total reorientation, a difficult but fascinating process of self-discovery, in which he has already, though unknowingly, begun to engage with the reading of these lines of poetry. The teacher of English at the Lord Byron School has just become the sorcerer's apprentice at Bourani.

This excerpt from "Little Gidding" also suggests the principal means of Nicholas's new education. Conchis will stimulate Nicholas to "unceasing exploration." The cynic, who deceived himself into believing that his destiny is fixed and his self-image permanent, will realize that he and his world are still to be explored and discovered. And the rationalist will realize that reason alone is insufficient for his quest. The experience at Bourani ultimately serves to impress upon Nicholas what his narrative so forcefully impresses upon us, that, as Conchis says, "mystery has energy. It pours energy into whoever seeks the answer to it." But I anticipate.

Determined to meet the man, Nicholas returns to Bourani the following week, goes to the villa, and knocks on the door. Maurice Conchis appears in the doorway. His authority and decisiveness, coupled with his changeableness, unnerve the young man. His remarks are gnomic and cryptic, yet somehow appropriate and to the point. The confrontation has a shock effect on Nicholas. He remains in doubt on all issues. Conchis is like no one he has met before. His efforts to characterize the man (and so to imagine by this that

he knows him better) are exciting, though humorous
and clearly inadequate: perhaps he is mad, or "simply
an old queer," a transvestite, a spiritualist, perhaps an
illusionist? By allusion, Conchis associates himself with
Zeus and with Prospero. Nicholas notes a resemblance
to Picasso, later to Ghandi.

Because the portrait of Conchis is painted by
Nicholas, who himself is never certain about what is
actual and what is fabricated in the old man's past
and present life, the reader is never quite sure whether
Conchis is to be taken as charlatan or shaman. The
figure, however, does suggest a paradigm of the civilized person: cosmopolitan (half English and half
Greek by birth), a man of great wealth and personal
magnetism, an entrepreneur, a patron of the arts,
musician, "psychic," scholar, one-time scientist and
physician, and apparent actor-manager of a versatile
improvisational acting troupe. His name carries an
obvious pun on "conscious(ness)" and his domain,
Bourani, as he says, is the old Albanian pirates' slang
for "skull." (It must be noted here, however, that
Fowles insists that the pun on consciousness was un-
intentional. He told me that the name was formed
from "conch," by which he meant to suggest "echo-
catching, sea-murmuring" qualities. The reader may
take his choice—or take them both.)

These symbolic names, in combination with the
geographical metaphors discussed above, already provide more than sufficient indication that the journey
from London to Phraxos and back to London is a
journey of self-discovery, to be interpreted as both
external and internal reality. It is at once a physical
reality, that is, an actual journey over space and time,
and a metaphorical account of a nonphysical, experi-
ential reality, that other kind of trip over the inner
landscape of the mind.

One of the first things that Conchis explains to Nicholas is how he came to Bourani, how, when he saw the place, he knew he must stay:

There comes a time in each life like a point of fulcrum. At that time you must accept yourself. It is not any more what you will become. It is what you are and always will be. You are too young to know this. You are still becoming. Not being.

If one does not recognize one's "point of fulcrum," one will be "like the many. Only the few recognize this moment. And act on it." With these words, the Magus impresses the notion of the "elect" upon the mind of his young protégé. Nicholas's experience at Bourani is designed to bring him to a complete understanding of this central and recurring image of the point of fulcrum, and of the need to act upon what he knows. Nicholas's story is the account of his initiation into the secret world of the elect, the meaning of the ordeals and rituals, and their impact upon his life.

The Magus alternately impresses, baffles, and frightens his student, but the overall effect of the encounter is precisely what Nicholas needs at the moment, a feeling of anticipation and enthusiasm, the feeling that he "wanted to live again." Nicholas returns each weekend. Each time he hears another installment of the master's "autobiography," a spellbinding tale that spans the two great wars, extends over much of the globe, and contains the events that have supposedly shaped his life and some that have shaped modern history.

In conjunction with these installments come mysterious epiphanies involving figures or episodes from Conchis's life story, or from history or mythology. Nicholas quickly feels himself "deep in the strangest maze in Europe," involved in "a game within a game within a game." This "strange new meta-theater," as

Conchis calls it at one point, has no curtain and no
audience, and demands that all who participate be
actors. Bourani appears to be "a world without limits,"
a manipulated reality in which nothing is entirely
credible, but in which anything seems possible and
permitted.

"I was trying to tell a fable," says Fowles, "about
the relationship between man and his conception of
God."[9] For Fowles, Conchis remains an abstract fig-
ure: "he's really a collocation of abstract ideas, rather
uneasily squashed into one . . . really he was meant
to be stages of the human attitude towards God."[10]
Conchis's identity, his true motives, and deeper purpose, therefore, remain elusive and enigmatic. Like
God in today's world, he offers Nicholas few clues:
"No certainties. No sights. No reasons. No motives."
It is not without interest that, before publication,
Fowles's alternative titles for the novel were "The
Maze" and "The Godgame."[11] As Nicholas learns at
the end, the other participants in the Bourani experience refer to it as "the godgame." In the foreword to
the revised edition, Fowles mentions that he still sometimes regrets having rejected "The Godgame" as the
title, and he enlarges upon what he meant by attitude
toward God: "human illusions about something that
does not exist in fact, absolute knowledge and absolute
power. The destruction of such illusions seems to me
still an eminently humanist aim."

Gradually the mysteries take on a dynamic, se-
quential form—a plot in literary or dramatic terms—
blending with Nicholas's life and linking it with
Conchis's, forming what the participants refer to as
the masque. (A masque is a form of dramatic enter-
tainment, in England associated primarily with the
seventeenth century, which deals largely with mythological, fantastic, or pastoral figures, and in which
song, dance, lavish costume, and spectacle often take

precedence over dialogue and plot development. The reader may remember the elaborate masque directed by Prospero in Act IV of *The Tempest*, a play more than once alluded to in *The Magus*.) Nicholas, against his rational will, is drawn deeper and deeper into the masque of Conchis and his players. As the roles and episodes proliferate, as the dark meaning of the action becomes progressively more complex and personally relevant to him, Nicholas tries harder and harder to expose and analyze the masque, to reduce it to a manageable, explicable reality. Everything, however, seems designed to disorient him, to undermine his rationalist approach. The distinctions between illusion and reality, between art and life, become increasingly blurred. Conchis, like a Zen master, sets up then smashes one illusion after another. Nicholas, his fortunate dupe, is coerced into participating until he is stripped of illusion, until he is brought to the knowledge and acceptance of himself for the first time.

So Nicholas plays the Fool to Conchis's Magus, the most important symbolic relationship of the novel. The epigraph to *The Magus*, taken from Arthur Edward Waite's *The Key to the Tarot*, informs us that the Magus is a figure borrowed from the Tarot, a deck of seventy-eight symbolic cards: fifty-six in four suits, the forerunner of our modern playing cards, called the Minor or Lesser Arcana; and twenty-two other picture cards, called the Major or Greater Arcana. The symbolism of the Major Arcana is a kind of mystical and metaphysical shorthand. Each of the twenty-two cards represents a power, a law, or a principle of the cosmos. The first (or last in some systems), numbered zero, is the Fool; the second, Roman numeral one, is the Magus or Magician.

According to Waite, the Magus is the "adept," the human reflection of God, the man who possesses the knowledge and power to manifest the cosmic truth on earth. The Fool is "the spirit in search of experience," although "conventional explanations say that the Fool signifies the flesh, the sensitive life."[12] The Magus is at one with the world. He draws the world into himself and imposes himself on the world. The Fool does the opposite: he separates himself by objectifying and depersonalizing the world; he estranges himself, through rationalism and skepticism, from the "magic" of his human and natural environment.

Throughout the story, Nicholas refers to himself as Conchis's "fool," or "dupe." In the only poem that the would-be poet writes after arriving at Bourani, Nicholas's self-image is that of the Fool (pictured on the card as standing, apparently unconcerned, at the edge of a precipice):

> From this skull-rock strange golden roots throw
> Ikons and incidents; the man in the mask
> Manipulates. I am the fool that falls
> And never learns to wait and watch,
> Icarus eternally, damned, the dupe of time . . . .

Instead of falling to his death, the Fool descends into the abyss of manifestation and judgment. He passes through the experiences suggested by some of the other symbols of the Greater Arcana in order to become a Magus, or one who knows and accepts the World, the naked dancer (Alison) whose image is the last, number XXI, of the Greater Arcana.

The Fool and the Magus are the alpha and omega of human experience.[13] The Fool is the occult representative of the Many. In his sack he carries the magical symbols of the wand, cup, sword, and pentacle, but he has no understanding of their meaning and power. He is ignorant until he learns of the potential which is man's, and impotent until he can act on this knowledge. When he knows, he gains self-mastery; when he acts, he becomes master of his world. In these terms,

Nicholas's growing self-awareness and self-acceptance may be seen as the evolution from Fool to Magus, what has previously been referred to as the destiny of the "elect."

Memories of Alison punctuate Nicholas's experiences at Bourani, especially as he continually contrasts her with the beautiful and enchanting young woman who, along with Nicholas, co-stars in the masque. This mysterious woman first appears as the "ghost," in Edwardian costume, of Conchis's dead fiancée, Lily Montgomery ("the dead live by love," Conchis tells Nicholas). Nicholas suspects that she is Conchis's mistress. Conchis later tells him that she is a dangerous schizophrenic, role-playing for therapy. She says she is an innocent English girl, Julie Holmes, selected by the old man to take the part of Lily, but beginning to be frightened by his weird and uncertain demands. That Nicholas wants to fall in love with her is clear, as is the fact that she wants him to. The figure of Lily-Julie, the temptress and the tease, is pure invention, in every way the antithesis of the absent Alison, who, as Conchis suggests, is cast as "Reality" in the masque. This figure embodies the stereotype of the ungraspable feminine ideal, invented to show Nicholas the true effect of his masculine sexual fantasies.

The situation is even further complicated by the appearance of a second Lily-Julie—her twin sister, Rose-June. The twin's part in the novel is small (although enlarged in the revised version), and it is on Lily that Nicholas focuses his attention.

At the point when Nicholas admits to himself that he is bewitched by the masque and enchanted by Lily, Alison re-appears on the scene to introduce the very important element of reality into Nicholas's life. Alison writes to Nicholas explaining that she can manage a few days' vacation, and Nicholas, only with the greatest reluctance, goes to Athens to meet her. For him she is merely "something that could be used if nothing better turned up." Sex with Alison is unthinkable for our deluded young hero, who feels that he must remain "faithful" to Lily—or rather to his self-imposed illusion of her. As usual, he lies to Alison, this time telling her that he has contracted syphilis (by now he has been disabused of his earlier illusion—Conchis told him that he had the common "soft sore" and was duped by his physicians). Always what Alison does is set against what Nicholas fantasizes a purer Lily might do.

They decide to leave Athens and to climb Mount Parnassus. The exhilaration of the ascent, the serenity and grandeur of the site, the memory of shared experiences in the past, all naturally combine to bring the couple closer together. On Parnassus, the mountain of poets, he thought "her unsubtlety, her inability to hide behind metaphor," would offend him, would bore him like "uncomplex poetry." But these qualities prove to be her true strength, for Nicholas realizes that Alison always had the ability to slip through the obstacles he placed between them, to "evoke deep similarities, to annul, or to make shallow, the differences in taste or feeling."

Descending the mountain, they come upon a little clearing, at first only casually compared to Eden, but in which Nicholas has a sudden vision of Alison with the innocence of Eve: "I was seeing through all the ugly, the unpoetic accretions of modern life to the naked real self. . . . Eve glimpsed again through ten thousand generations." The simple fact that he has loved her all the time rushes in upon him, as does the other fact that he is still incapable of relinquishing his attachment to Lily. Alison offers him an ultimatum foreshadowing the one he will offer her at the end, the direct choice of "yes or no," whether or not to assume the responsibility of living with someone who loves

him. Nicholas says no, perhaps aided in his decision
by Alison's brutal analysis of his character:

I think you're so blind you probably don't even know . . .
you're a filthy selfish bastard who can't, can't like being
impotent, can't *ever* think of anything except number one.
Because nothing can hurt you, Nicko. Deep down, where
it counts. You've built your life so that nothing can ever
reach you. So whatever you do you can say, I couldn't
help it. You can't lose. You can always have your next
adventure. Your next bloody affaire.

This speech provides the reader, long before it
does Nicholas, with the main clue to the reason for,
and the nature of, the masque. Alison's words, however forceful, however accurate, cannot reach Nicholas
"deep down, where it counts." They cannot break
the spell of separation under which he lives. This is
the function of the Magus, the one who dramatizes the
metaphors of experience when words will not suffice.
Sometimes, as Carlos Castaneda remarks in *A Separate
Reality*, one must be *tricked* into becoming a man of
knowledge.
It is Conchis and company who finally manage
to penetrate the illusions of his ego fortress, exposing
his romantic self-dramatization for what it actually is.
Before Nicholas encounters Conchis, he knows himself
only through the fabrication he has created to deceive
himself. The masque, especially in its climactic scenes,
serves to destroy this fiction, allowing for a painful
confrontation with himself and the resurrection of his
long-buried power to relate fully to others. Seen in this
way, the masque amounts to a kind of psychodrama,
and Conchis to a kind of psychotherapist.
Not long after the Parnassus episode—representing, perhaps, Reality's intermission in the masque—
Nicholas is led to believe that Alison has committed
suicide, the very deed that he was not authentic

enough to perform. The shock of the news sparks the sudden and profound realization of his (man's, more generally) narcissistic brutality: "My monstrous crime was Adam's, the oldest and most vicious of all male selfishnesses: to have imposed the role I needed from Alison on her real self." Her loss, however, also has the effect of driving Nicholas even deeper into the masque in search of solace and release from his terrible responsibility. His is the "characteristically twentieth-century retreat from content into form, from meaning into appearance, from ethics into aesthetics."

The attainment of Lily now seems a necessity, though he is still unaware that he is actually enamored only of his own onanistic fantasy of woman. His inclination remains Adam's, to body forth a part of himself in order to fulfill a need in himself. The woman for whom Nicholas believes he has fallen is a fantasy figure who will be "trained by familiarity, by love . . . to do all those things that Alison did." Later, when Nicholas is made to believe that his superior intelligence has brought the masque to an abrupt and abortive conclusion, he begins to prepare the scenario for his enjoyment of Julie. He will take her with "a gentle roughness, a romantic brutality"; he will "celebrate" Alison in Julie, remeet and remake her. This entirely fanciful consummation is to be followed by a less-than-complete confession about Alison, which in turn, he can even bring himself to imagine, will be followed by marriage.

After teasing, tempting, and tormenting him in what has been called the definitive fictional example of *coitus interruptus*,[14] she announces that "there is no Julie." At this moment the masque starts up again with a vengeance. The door flies open, and two of the actors bind, gag, and drug the enraged and humiliated lover. The conscious portrayal of the traitress was but a reflection of the role that Nicholas has played for

years, and, in this respect, Julie is no more than the
artful objectification of Nicholas's selfish manipulation of others. The painful process of disillusionment
begins here with the betrayer betrayed. The climactic
scenes, however, are yet to come: the trial, judgment,
and "disintoxication."

After three days, Nicholas awakens from his
narcosis. He is again gagged and escorted to a large
underground chamber, the walls of which are decorated
with arcane emblems. This is the "courtroom," and
Nicholas, the "judge and executioner," is given the
throne of honor. Thirteen participants, dressed in gro-
tesque occult costumes, take their seats before him.
They unmask, revealing the major participants in the
Bourani experience along with a few others, and they
rather unconvincingly explain that the previous cha-
rades constituted a secret experiment in behavioral
research. Nicholas is then subjected to a very clever
parody of a psychoanalytic exposition of his personality. He is taunted with his emotional and psychic
debilities. He is diagnosed as a person who has re-
gressed to an infantile state in which he is dominated
by self-gratification needs. To achieve satisfaction of
these needs, he is driven futilely by an unconscious
repetition compulsion. Although there is much truth in
the analysis, it is ultimately inadequate as an explanation of Nicholas's behavior. Its primary function is as a
ritual device to humiliate and degrade him even further.

It is his tormentors, however, who are on trial.
Nicholas must judge them and punish the scapegoat
they have chosen, Dr. Vanessa Maxwell, the brave and
brilliant young psychiatrist who played the role of
Lily-Julie in their experiment. Her wrists are hand-
cuffed to a flogging frame, her back is bared. Nicholas
is given a cat-o-nine-tails and the absolute freedom to
administer up to ten strokes. The choice to inflict pain,
he is told, will demonstrate the "satisfactory comple-

tion of [his] disintoxication." He feels, of course, that he will be "judged by [his] own judgment," that this is the ultimate existential moment. He recalls the climactic moment of Conchis's autobiography, when the older man had been confronted with a similar choice, the execution of a mutilated Cretan terrorist on Nazi-occupied Phraxos. To Conchis, the terrorist personified the unchangeable essence of freedom, the "final right to deny," "the freedom to do all [which] stood against only one thing—the prohibition not to do all." He realizes, as Conchis did, that his freedom lies in not striking his victim. As he drops the whip, Nicholas senses a moment of mutual respect among all of the participants in this bizarre ritual. He has the "dim conviction of having entered some deeper, wiser esoteric society."

Because he has chosen not to punish, Nicholas is forced to play one more role. This time it is he who is fastened to the flogging frame, to be subjected to a metaphorical flogging amounting to a final disintoxication with Lily-Julie and all that she represents for him. In psychiatric terms, this scene is analogous to a highly imaginative withdrawal therapy. He is treated to a blue movie starring "the Fabulous Whore," known also as the romantic Edwardian virgin, Lily Montgomery; the contemporary college co-ed, Julie Holmes; the learned Dr. Vanessa Maxwell; and the mythological triune goddess, Astarte, the "mother of mystery," and, incidentally, the figure to whom Fowles has dedicated *The Magus*.

Then the screen is removed and the curtains drawn to reveal a stage. Like a crucified Iago, Nicholas is forced to witness in the flesh his idealized white virgin copulating with her black lover. The curtain is closed. Conchis appears to tell Nicholas that he is now "elect." His ordeal of initiation has been successfully completed. It is only after this final disintoxication that

Nicholas can take stock of himself and ask his variation of the ancient Greek question. "What was I?" he
asks, and his response represents a significant milestone in his developing self-awareness:

Exactly what Conchis had had me told: nothing but the
net sum of countless wrong turnings. Why? I dismissed
most of the Freudian jargon of the trial; but all my life I
had tried to turn life into fiction, to hold reality away;
always I had acted as if a third person was watching and
listening and giving me marks for good or bad behavior—
a god like a novelist, to whom I turned, like a character
with the power to please, the sensitivity to feel slighted,
the ability to adapt himself to whatever he believed the
novelist-god wanted. This leechlike variation of the super-
ego I had created myself, fostered myself, and because
of it I had always been incapable of acting freely. It was
not my defense, but my despot.

The masque has supposedly concluded, but Nicholas continues to search out its meaning and Conchis
apparently continues to plant clues and to assign roles.
Nicholas is dismissed from the Lord Byron School. He
discovers that Alison is alive, that even "her crystal
core of non-betrayal" was his illusion. She must have
agreed to join the masque, but at what point and precisely why remain unexplained.

Part III contains the return to England and concludes with the rediscovery of Alison. Nicholas has
seen the masque through to its curtain scene, and he
is in the process of translating its metaphors into a
personal vision of life. The third part of the novel
constitutes a detective game. There is a further un-
ravelling of the plot and an attempt to fit together the
remaining pieces of the puzzle. This is combined with
a kind of psychic purgatorial experience, in which
Nicholas undergoes a period of further introspection
while waiting for Alison to appear.

He has two important guides for this last part of
his journey. A pre-arranged one is Mrs. Lily de Seitas,
the human prototype for the fictitious Lily Montgomery, the real-life mother of the twins, and a person Nicholas identifies with the mythological Demeter,
mother earth. A mother figure is just as important for
Nicholas now as the temptress was before. She offers
him sympathy and prescription, which he is finally
able to assimilate: first, "the one thing that must never
come between two people who have offered each other
love is a lie"; second, "thou shalt not commit pain"
(emended in the revised version to "thou shalt not
inflict unnecessary pain").

His second guide, unwitting and fortuitous, is
Jojo, an unattractive teenage bohemian from Glasgow.
He proposes two or three weeks of companionship—
"no sex. Just companionship"—and she accepts. From
the imagery he uses to describe her, it seems that
Nicholas conceives of her as a faithful dog, man's
best companion (she has an innocent "puppy grin,"
she is "grateful for the smallest bone, like an old mon-
grel," etc.). Jojo, of course, falls in love with him.
Surely the main deficiency in the characterization of
Nicholas lies in his attraction for the females of the
novel when he seems to have none whatsoever for the
reader.

Whereas Mrs. de Seitas instructs Nicholas by
precept, Jojo provides the example. As Jojo slips perfectly into the role he has cast for her, Nicholas
realizes that once again he has committed the primal
sin of man. He has abused her love and her innocence;
he has treated her as he has treated all of her prede-
cessors, like a utilizable object. Despite his selfish
blindness, however, they do grow emotionally close,
close enough, at least, for her to provide an ear for
Nicholas's by now long-overdue confession. Jojo's main

psychic function here is as "the strangest priest to confess before; but not the worst. For she absolved me."

Shortly after this incident Nicholas's landlady, known simply as Kemp, takes him for a late-afternoon walk. She vanishes and Alison appears, simply and without drama, staring across a table at the tea pavilion in Regent's Park. Having imagined himself in the role of Orpheus in search of Eurydice, Nicholas is disappointed with the lack of theatricality in Alison's "entrance." He believes that he is still the star of the show, that the masquers are spying on them, that this is but another playlet after an extended interval. He constructs a short, open-ended script for Alison to improvise with her own choice. (This also has been cut in the revision.) He slaps her, they part, she will take a cab to the waiting room of Paddington Station where they will meet, she will contact no one. Or she will not meet him, she will return to Australia or at least "some Australia of the mind" without him. "But you don't say yes or no. You do yes or no," a reworking of Alison's ultimatum to him on Parnassus, an echo of Conchis facing the Greek freedom fighter and Nicholas facing the bare back of Lily. "Her turn to know" the cruelty and responsibility of freedom.

Then suddenly he realizes:

There were no watching eyes. The windows were as blank as they looked. The theater was empty. It was not a theater. They had told her it was a theater, and she had believed them, and I had believed her. To bring us to this —not for themselves, but for us.

The actor-manager has absented himself from the afterpiece, taking his players and his properties with him. Nicholas is left to his own resources, to do with his life what he will. This is the moment of truth toward which the entire course of events has led, the

moment that Nicholas, harking back to Conchis's
earlier simile, rightly identifies as "our point of
fulcrum."

What happens after this is "another mystery." An
ending, we are told, is "no more than a point in sequence, a snip of the cutting shears." Whether or not
the lovers are united is a matter only for conjecture,
though the Latin lines with which the novel concludes
suggest a positive attitude regardless of the outcome
of this particular match: "He who has never loved, let
him love tomorrow; and he who has loved, let him
(also) love tomorrow." With regard to the ending,
Richard B. Stolley relates the following anecdote:

In response to a gentle letter from a New York lawyer,
dying of cancer in a hospital, who said he very much
wanted the couple to be reunited, Fowles wrote back,
"yes, of course, they were." On the same day he got a
"horrid" letter from an American woman who angrily de-
manded, "Why can't you say what you mean, and for God's
sake, what happened in the end?" Fowles replied curtly:
"They never saw each other again."[15]

Conchis asserts that questions are life-supporting,
answers a form of death. The fact that the open-ended
conclusion leaves the reader with an unanswerable
question suggests that the structure of The Magus is
designed to enact the truth that the Magus proclaims.
What participation in the masque does for Nicholas,
the reading of the novel can do for us. We must here
participate in constructing the plot and interpreting
character. As E. M. Forster remarked in a slightly
different context and about a greater novel (War and
Peace), the idea the novelist must cling to is not "completion" but "expansion," "not rounding off but opening
out."[16] The emphasis of The Magus is quite clearly on
beginnings, not endings; on the moment of choice
initiating action, not on the outcome of that action. It

is the quest that the novel promotes, not the destination; living in the labyrinth of life and deriving strength from its mysteries, not finding a way out.

The Magus remains an enormously complex and ambitious work, all the more remarkable as it is Fowles's first effort in fiction. It is eclectic and synthetic, associative and densely allusive. Woven together to create its intricate fabric are the elements of a variety of literary forms, including the thriller, the Gothic novel, the traditional quest story, the erotic romance, and the philosophical novel. The straightforward realism of Part I, to which Fowles returns in Part III, is, in the huge second section, abandoned for exuberant fantasy and undisguised allegory. The social interest of the early pages gives way with the realistic illusion to the occult and mythic concerns of Part II. In addition to this stylistic variety, *The Magus* touches upon much that is central to the thought and feeling of the age, echoing many of the voices that have shaped our time.

This extraordinary amalgam of content and styles still manages to function as a relatively cohesive whole. To begin with, everything in *The Magus* happens to, or for the sake of, the protagonist, and everything is related from his point of view. No matter how bewildering the events become, Nicholas is always the consistent focus for them. Already discussed are the key ideas and problems introduced early in the novel and enlarged or developed through its numerous episodes. There are abundant examples of the meaningful repetition of key word and phrases, such as "freedom," "choice," "mystery," "return," "waiting room," "someone watching," and so on. Woven throughout the text, they form complex patterns of imagery and cohesive structural and thematic elements. *The Magus* becomes a kind of echo chamber in which these elements are made to reverberate powerfully and dynamically, accruing meaning with each occurrence and association. Sometimes key statements are reflected in the action, as when, for example, Nicholas experiences an event similar to one referred to by Conchis in the course of one of his monologues. Sometimes the process is reversed, that is to say, an experience will later find its verbal counterpart.

That *The Magus* manages to gain unity and cohesion does not mean that it does not also suffer from certain stylistic and structural defects. At times harmony of design does seem to have been sacrificed for inclusiveness of subject matter, and clarity for self-conscious ingenuity. The language—especially the existentialist jargon—is sometimes pretentious beyond the demands of the situations which it articulates. The themes do not require quite so much exposition and mystification. There is definitely too much hocus-pocus, even for an experienced magician, and Fowles seems to overindulge his delight in playing with the reader, in leading him down blind alleys to dead ends. There are words and thoughts too obviously and unnecessarily repeated (though these are largely rectified in the revised edition).

There are gratuitous incidents and, more significantly, gratuitous characters (one might point to Lily's double, Rose-June, perhaps even to the landlady, Kemp). Other troublesome aspects of characterization remain: the discrepancy between Nicholas's unattractiveness to us and his appeal to the women in the novel has already been noted, as has the omission of Alison's motive for joining the masque and the details of her collaboration. More on Conchis's aims and his network of information could have been provided without diminishing the force of the man's mysterious presence. As the character stands now, his symbolic roles are more credible than his realistic one. That is, because of the gaps in our understanding of his actions and motives, it is not easy to believe in the eccentric millionaire as a credible character at the realistic level of interpretation.

Fowles's own critical dissatisfaction with the novel is evinced by the hundreds upon hundreds of lexical and other minor stylistic emendations that affect, in one way or another, nearly every chapter of the revised edition. The revision, however, seems not especially designed to meet the broader criticisms of structure and style voiced by many of Fowles's original reviewers (especially across the Atlantic). They might still object to the union of disparate elements, the overly complex artifice, and the self-conscious pyrotechnics.

No new characters have been introduced and none have been removed. However, the role of Julie's twin sister has been given greater prominence and other characters have undergone more subtle changes. Despite the fact that the text has been somewhat enlarged, its structure and story-line remain relatively unchanged. The first and third parts, with the exception of the concluding chapter, remain very much the same, while everywhere in Part II there are significant alterations. Nothing seems to have escaped Fowles's scrutiny here, the emendations extending to details of costume, gesture, and setting, even to the short notes exchanged among the various characters. The overall effect of these changes has been to tighten the style, up-date the references, provide greater verisimilitude to the events, and establish greater credibility for the characters and their actions.

Some half dozen chapters in Part II have been entirely re-written. The scenes at Bourani have undergone the most radical revision, especially in terms of the dialogue, which, although somewhat expanded, is less repetitive and more economical. The erotic element has been made more explicit and contemporary, perhaps reflecting the change of social and literary values in the 1970s, perhaps indicating a greater self-confidence in the author. Two new, explicitly sexual scenes between Nicholas and Julie have been created: a magnificent naked night swim replaces their frustrated embraces in chapter 49; and a stunning sexual climax in chapter 58 replaces the exasperating interruption originally in chapter 59. This last addition is particularly significant, for it was the absence of consummation which characterized the original relationship of Nicholas and Julie and which created the tensions and rhythms of the plot.

The epigraph from *The Key to the Tarot* and the dedication "To Astarte" have been removed in the revised edition, thus suggesting from the outset the de-emphasis of the arcane material and the de-mystification of some of the events. At the same time, there has been a new emphasis placed on the psychological meaning of those events through increased reference to psychological details. Despite the clever and more frequent parallels with *The Tempest* in the second version, Conchis is less the magus and more the psychiatrist. Fowles mentions Jungian psychology in the foreword as an obvious influence on the novel and Conchis specifically mentions that he studied under Jung. More stress is given to the psychological —as distinct from theatrical—nature of Conchis's experiment. He is supposedly a professor emeritus at the Sorbonne, working with a new therapeutic technique called "situational therapy." This experiment allows him to apply his life-long interest in the "delusional symptoms of insanity" to sane subjects as well as insane.

Although all of these details are fabricated, it is still clear that the other participants in the experiment have great confidence in the abilities of the master. It is also made clear to Nicholas that the events at

Bourani have been staged for him, though the precise motivation is still not revealed. More stress is placed on Julie's schizophrenic role, less on her historical and theatrical ones. These alterations taken together provide a sharper focus for the events and relationships at Bourani. Conchis also gains further credibility on the realistic level.

Although the role of the occult has been slightly diminished, the religious parody has been presented with greater clarity and in greater detail. The allusions to God in the now "fundamentally benevolent" figure of Conchis have been strengthened. The new foreword indicates Fowles's desire to clarify his original intentions in this regard. "I did intend Conchis," he writes, "to exhibit a series of masks representing human notions of God, from the supernatural to the jargon-ridden scientific." The relationship of God and man's freedom, which is developed in *The Aristos,* is restated here: "God and freedom are totally antipathetic concepts; and men believe in their imaginary gods most often because they are afraid to believe in the other thing."

Finally, the concluding moments of the novel have been rewritten. The new ending has been made less ambiguous and more conciliatory, perhaps in response to the numerous inquiries Fowles has received from his disappointed and perplexed readers. Changing the ending in this way, however, seems less in keeping with the general philosophy of the work, with the insistence on maintaining the quest and deferring the goal. The first paragraph of the final chapter still includes leaving the "anti-hero" "at a crossroads, in a dilemma," with "no direction, no reward; because we too are waiting . . . for this girl, this truth . . . to return; and to say she returns is a lie." Now, however, these key concepts have less relevance to the conclusion. There is a reward, there is a direction, and Alison seems to have returned.

The other very important alteration in the final pages involves the excision of certain images which I have previously noted as recurrent: "the waiting room," the "point of fulcrum," *eleutheriá* (Greek for "freedom"), and the slap that initiates the moment of Alison's crucial choice—recalling the parallel incidents of the lovers on Parnassus, Conchis on Nazi-occupied Phraxos, and Nicholas at the trial. Exactly why Fowles has cut these echoes is not clear, but their loss seems to me regrettable. They provided a neat, economical, and unobtrusive recapitulation of some of the central concepts and events of the novel. The new ending is more a conclusion to the tale, but less a summation of theme and image.

As Fowles remarks in his foreword, *The Magus*— like Alain-Fournier's *Le Grand Meaulnes,* which had so profound an influence on the first draft—remains "a novel of adolescence written by a retarded adolescent." While this self-analysis is far from the whole truth, it does shed light on the novel and on an important characteristic of Fowles's fiction more generally. *The Magus, The Collector,* certainly the novella, "The Ebony Tower," and (to a lesser extent) *The French Lieutenant's Woman* are "adolescent" in their exclusive fixation on the vision of the individual ego asserting itself in the world. They tend too often to limit individual experience to choices between extremes. They too often reduce the meaning of human interactions to matters black and white, without the vast range of shades and shadows that we all recognize. They rarely include the virtues of the difficult, sometimes necessary accommodations and compromises that "mature" individuals, living together in the real world, feel it is their responsibility or their duty to make. This adolescent vision (if indeed this is the proper term) is outgrown with the creation of *Daniel Martin*, a novel which may well prove a turning point in Fowles's career, and which we shall examine in the final chapter.

Fowles's admirers too frequently have become idolators. At the risk of seeming to join their ranks, and in the face of the author's own self-denigration, as well as the critical reservations expressed above, I still concur with one, perhaps over-zealous, reviewer, that *The Magus* does represent "a highly interesting attempt to write the Great English Novel."[17] It misses only by the skin of its young author's teeth.

4

The French Lieutenant's Woman

I met a lady in the meads
  Full beautiful, a faery's child;
Her hair was long, her foot was light,
  And her eyes were wild.
        —John Keats, "La Belle Dame
        Sans Merci," Stanza 4

The ultimate tension: between knowledge and
what will never be known by the knower—
that is, mystery. —*The Aristos*[1]

The two previous novels were popular successes, especially in the United States where *The Magus* became
something of a cult novel among the young. Nevertheless, it was only with the publication of *The French
Lieutenant's Woman* that Fowles's work appeared as
a best seller on both sides of the Atlantic and that his
reputation was extended into the more rarified atmosphere of academe. The sales of the paperback edition
are rapidly approaching the 3,000,000 mark, while
those of *The Magus* lag just slightly behind.[2]

The intrinsic historical interest of *The French
Lieutenant's Woman,* coupled with its typically contemporary structural and stylistic experimentation,
have attracted a discriminating readership. The study
of nineteenth-century sources and influences, illuminating the meaning of the novel and the method of the

author, has also attracted considerable scholarly attention.[3] The wealth of allusion, both explicit and veiled,
to Victorian life and thought, the constant echoes of
nineteenth-century fiction and poetry, and the many
stylistic parodies will go largely unnoticed by readers
who are not at least somewhat familiar with Victorian
literature.

The French Lieutenant's Woman represents a
quite considerable exercise of historical imagination,
a talent Fowles already exhibited in the historical
reflections and digressions of *The Magus*. Fowles is
steeped in the social and political history of nineteenth-
century England and, perhaps more important, in its
imaginative literature. In *The French Lieutenant's
Woman*, he has succeeded in providing an intimate
and accurate evocation of the third quarter of that
century, the so-called Victorian Golden Age. Both high
society and life below stairs are portrayed with equal
facility. Costume, manners, and decor are described
with precision, while the dialogue Fowles has invented seems their perfect complement.

There is a wealth of geographical and topographical detail, seascapes and landscapes, rural and urban
scenes alike. The novel ranges from domestic life in
Dorset to the seamier parts of London, from the rec-
reations of the masses and the popular taste of the day
to its central moral and philosophical questions. It
dramatizes many of the social concerns of Victorian
England, especially the great changes in social structure involved in the emergence of a wealthy and
powerful commercial class, the demise of the aristoc-
racy, and the beginnings of female emancipation. This
is the age the historian G. M. Young has called "the
most striking example" in British history "of pacific,
creative, unsubversive revolution,"[4] and Fowles has
unearthed the seeds of that revolution in the social
structure, thought, and art of the time.

The French Lieutenant's Woman, however, is a historical novel of a special kind, and not at all in the sense of being based on particular historical figures or events, which here are mainly imaginary. Fowles has succeeded equally in illuminating the age of which he writes and the age *in* which he writes. The Victorian Golden Age is frequently compared with our own and each is used to shed light on the other. The author-narrator is deliberately, perhaps even too self-consciously, contemporary in his perspective on the earlier period and in the chronological scope of his reference. "I live in the age of Alain Robbe-Grillet and Roland Barthes," says he in his first personal intrusion into the nineteenth-century setting. During the course of his narrative, he refers to Freud, Hitler, Henry Moore, and Marshal McLuhan, to film, television, radar, the jet engine, and so on. Thus the reader is invited to enter an expertly depicted Victorian world, but constantly reminded that he is, after all, merely an observer from a great historical distance.

Fowles recreates not only the Victorian world, but the Victorian novel as well, and the juxtaposition of historical periods described above also has its stylistic counterpart. While the book provides an authentic pastiche of Victorian novelistic conventions, it also parodies those conventions and introduces some interesting variations on the most familiar structural features, especially the omniscient narrative voice. So *The French Lieutenant's Woman* is both a historical novel and an experimental one, aligned as much with the work of Alain Robbe-Grillet and Roland Barthes as with Charles Dickens, George Eliot, and Thomas Hardy. The tension between fiction and reality and between the historical past and the present are manipulated from the first page to the last.

＊　＊　＊

The setting is Lyme Regis on the Dorset coast, the same place in which John Fowles lives and writes today. From his workroom window, one can see in the distance the Dorset of Thomas Hardy, whose "shadow," says Fowles, "I cannot avoid,"[5] and whose influence is quite evident in the novel. Fowles takes many of the epigraphs heading each of the novel's sixty-one chapters from Hardy, and has occasion to refer to him in the course of the narrative. In his naturalist's eye for detail and in his topographical description, he is Hardy's disciple, perhaps even his rival. Hardy, alone among the Victorians, provides Fowles with some help in describing scenes of sexual passion, and the figure of the French Lieutenant's Woman, Sarah Woodruff, owes something to Hardy's heroines.[6]

The year is 1867, exactly a century before Fowles began writing the novel. This was the year in which Nobel invented dynamite and the first volume of Marx's *Das Kapital* appeared; it was the year in which the Paris World Fair introduced Japanese art to Europe, the British Parliament passed the second great Reform Bill, the British North America Act established the Dominion of Canada, and the United States purchased Alaska. The year's events provide a paradigm of the dynamic changes that occurred during the entire period, changes that are also reflected in the life of the hero of the novel.

On a blustery morning in late March of this year, two lovers, "of a very superior taste as regards their outward appearance," are seen walking the ancient Cobb, "the most beautiful sea rampart on the south coast of England." On the seaward end of the Cobb, leaning against an old, upended cannon barrel, motionless, staring out to sea, there is another, less distinct figure, "more like a living memorial to the drowned, a figure from myth, than any proper fragment of the petty provincial day." Its plain black clothes are in sharp contrast to the stylish elegance of the couple slowly approaching, and especially to the strident colors of the modish lady.

The first visual image is of Lyme Bay, the next is of the Cobb, then the town, then back again to the Cobb with its three human figures. Seemingly described from the objective point of view of the Victorian novelist, and seen as if through the telescope of Lyme's "local spy," these pictures simultaneously suggest a modern, cinematic panorama of sea, rampart, and town, with long-shots of the three major participants in the story. From the outset, then, the style of the novel suggests its curious amalgam of the nineteenth and twentieth centuries.

This first chapter, entirely descriptive and nearly without action, pictorially and vividly sets the scene in terms of time and place. The second chapter, however, is written mainly in dialogue form, the telescopic lens, as it were, moving into sharper focus, eventually leading to close-ups of the faces of the three. As we learn from their conversation, the elegant couple, Charles Smithson and Ernestina Freeman, are betrothed, and are down from London visiting her good-natured, spinster Aunt Tranter. As they near the end of the promontory, the person Charles took to be a fisherman he now sees is a woman. Ernestina is (symbolically) shortsighted and can still only make out a "dark shape." She guesses that this must be "poor Tragedy," otherwise known as "the French Lieutenant's Woman" or whore, and briefly relates the Lyme gossip surrounding this dark figure. The woman has been seduced and abandoned by the French Lieutenant, but fortunately no child has issued from their union; it is said she waits by the sea for his return; she is "a little mad"; she is ostracized by the community.

When Charles approaches the poor woman to cau-

tion her against the strength of the squalls, she turns
to him and the aspect she presents remains indelibly
imprinted on his memory. Hers is not a "pretty" face
like Ernestina's, but an "unforgettable face," a "tragic
face." It is described here and elsewhere by its external
features which hint at unseen qualities, and by what
it unexpectedly lacks instead of what is in it. "Theirs
was the age when the favored feminine look was the
demure, the obedient, the shy," but there is nothing
of these qualities in the face that turns toward Charles.
"There was no artifice there, no hypocrisy, no hysteria,
no mask; and above all, no sign of madness." His
attention throughout the story is focused on her hair
(elsewhere "ravishingly alive," but here only "pulled
tight back inside the collar of the black coat") and on
her eyes, with their intensity and their power. "Her
stare was aimed like a rifle at the farthest horizon."
Charles feels as though she looks "through him" instead of at him. The look is felt "as a lance," suggesting
her defense against his intrusion on her privacy, as well
as the familiar image of love's arrow.

This first encounter of no more than two or three
seconds makes him feel "an unjust enemy; both pierced
and deservedly diminished." Later Charles will sense
Sarah's presumption of intellectual equality. She will
come to embody those feminine qualities generally
repressed in the Victorian Age: passion, imagination,
and independence. Although we do not realize this
until the end, Sarah is quite consistently described as
an early prototype of the liberated woman. The second
chapter concludes with Charles expressing his wish
that Ernestina had not told him "the sordid facts."
"That's the trouble with provincial life," he says, reminiscent of Nicholas Urfe in *The Magus,* "everyone
knows everyone and there is no mystery. No romance."
Or so, like Nicholas, he thinks.

When one reflects upon all that the opening pages

of a novel must do—seize the reader's attention, establish the setting and situation, introduce the characters, launch the action, establish the identity of the narrator, and so on—and upon the very short distance we have come in this novel (the two chapters are but six pages together), it is remarkable how economically and effectively Fowles has achieved his ends. He has established the pattern which will dominate the plot and the rhythm of its action, a pattern, familiar to us from *The Magus,* of frequently undermined expectations, continuous disillusionment, and the very slow parcelling out of information vital to an understanding of character motivation. The reader will be as manipulated by the narrator as the hero is by the heroine.

The mystery and fascination of the title character have also been established, as have her isolation and elusiveness. The impression created by Sarah Woodruff is given to us from the perspective of Charles, a technique generally maintained throughout. We cannot miss the implicit contrast of Sarah and Ernestina, suggesting quite different levels of involvement for the hero. This contrast is also maintained and reinforced. As we shall soon see, it is only the first of the contrasts and parallels set up among the major actors in the drama.

These three characters form the love triangle on which the main plot is based. That another encounter between Charles and Sarah is destined to occur must be felt by all from the outset. That it is delayed for another eight chapters helps to embue it with the mysterious and romantic possibilities Charles so strongly feels are absent from provincial life. That he cannot remain satisfied with his intended spouse will be made plain from the various complications in the slowly developing plot, if the suggestion has not already been planted.

We should pause a little longer to note the emergence of one more character, albeit only in embryo. I refer to that other very important figure, unobtrusive at this point, who has been with us from the start, that changeable, whimsical, problematic, nameless Author-Narrator, known only by the pronoun "I." It is obvious that Fowles has taken great delight in his creation. An early allusion to Henry Moore lets us know immediately that he is our contemporary, though he often pretends to be a contemporary of Charles. He usually employs the familiar voice of the omniscient narrator of Victorian fiction and maintains a lively, learned, sometimes pedantic commentary on the characters and the events. He eventually enters his own story as a character in two different disguises: in chapter fifty-five, as the "massively bearded" evangelical type, unpleasantly self-confident, he is an unwelcome intruder into Charles's first-class train compartment on the way from Exeter to London; in the last chapter, in Chelsea, he appears as an "extremely important-looking," foppish and flashy impresario who regards the world as his theater to be used as he wills.

This charlatan has the audacity to claim to be the novelist himself, and, in chapter thirteen, draws the analogy between the novelist as creator and the Creator of the cosmos. However, conceived in the "new theological image" of "the freedom that allows other freedoms to exist," he claims to be a creator who respects the autonomy of the creatures of his mind, not the omniscient and authoritarian Victorian image of the god who controls his creatures. As we read *The French Lieutenant's Woman,* then, we must be on our guard for this nameless poseur, popping in and out of the story, breaking its illusion, and creating those dynamic tensions between fiction and history and between past and present, which characterize the novel.

Despite the title and the fact that the title character is called the protagonist, *The French Lieutenant's*

Woman is mainly about Charles Smithson, and chapter three is devoted exclusively to his person and to the family and social background from which he arises. Like Frederick Clegg and Nicholas Urfe before him, Charles is bereft of his parents. His mother died while bearing his still-born sister when Charles was less than two, and his father died "very largely of pleasure" when his son was twenty-one. Charles has since lived on his father's diminished fortune, but is now the sole heir to the baronetcy and the wealth of his ageing, but still vigorous, Uncle Robert.

When the story opens, Charles is thirty-two years of age. He has acquired considerable experience of life in England and abroad, certainly, at least, by comparison with the other figures we meet in Lyme, particularly the entirely innocent Ernestina, who is eleven years his junior. Charles has liberal sympathies, but no political ambitions. He is a "healthy agnostic" and an "intelligent idler."

The two foci of his intellectual interest loom larger and larger as the plot develops: Charles is one of the early though naive followers of Charles Darwin, and he has an enthusiastic and serious interest in paleontology and geology. Darwin's *Origin of Species* appeared in 1859 and the geologist, Sir Charles Lyell's *Antiquity of Man* in 1863 (Lyell's first great work, *The Principles of Geology,* having already been published in two volumes in 1830 and 1832). The intellectual revolution represented by the work of Darwin and Lyell was about to shake the very foundations of the Victorian structure, and this historical reality is clearly reflected in the personal interests and existential evolution of Charles Smithson.

In historical terms, *The French Lieutenant's Woman* has as its major concern the coming apart of the entire Victorian social fabric and the tentative beginnings of the modern age. From this vantage point, Charles's central characteristic is that he is "a man struggling to overcome history . . . even though he does not realize it." The tensions and contradictions within his character are, to a large extent, those of the Victorian Age, while the choices he makes throughout the story have the effect of bringing him much closer to ours. Fowles takes pains to show that out of the lost coherence of the period emerges new possibilities for the emancipation of humanity, that out of the personal and social upheavals comes a new potential for personal consciousness. The epigraph to the novel, from Marx's *Zur Judenfrage,* suggests these themes from the start: "Every emancipation is a restoration of the human world and of human relationships to man himself." Elsewhere, Fowles has remarked that his aim was "to show an existentialist awareness before it was chronologically possible."[7]

With chapter four, a sustained comic chapter close to Dickens in tone and portraiture, we return to the French Lieutenant's Woman, though only indirectly, through the description of her domestic environment, the household of Mrs. Poulteney. This splendid caricature is everything that Mrs. Tranter is not: an evangelical fanatic, a hypocrite, a tyrant, what we would call today an obsessive-compulsive character type in all matters relating to dirt (material and otherwise). Wanting to avoid the after-life of eternal damnation in which she so fervently believes, trying to assuage her feeling of wickedness in not having performed sufficient good deeds, Mrs. Poulteney wishes, as an act of "charity," to take a companion—"some refined person who has come upon adverse circumstances." To this end, she summons the vicar, Mr. Forsythe, who recommends, with "perhaps an emotion not absolutely unconnected with malice," Sarah Woodruff.

Chapter five is devoted to enlarging upon the person of Ernestina Freeman. She is contrasted with

Sarah, as the aunt she is staying with is contrasted with Mrs. Poulteney. Unlike Sarah, Ernestina is exactly what she seems, the possessor of all that the masculine society of her time required of its ladies. Hers is "exactly the right face for her age"—small-chinned, oval, pale, gentle. The look is one of innocence, delicacy, and obeisance, adulterated only by the faintest suggestion of an impish rebelliousness so alluring to a "modern man" like Charles. Ernestina is the spoiled, pampered, self-centered only child of a very wealthy London draper. She is amiable but tedious, intelligent though only conventionally so, sentimental as opposed to passionate. Her real attraction for Charles, we learn later, was "the ageless attraction of shallow-minded women: that one may make of them what one wants."

Following this chapter comes the second account of Sarah's romantic history (if we number Ernestina's few details as the first). It is Mr. Forsythe's, and he relates "some of what he knew"—but only some—to Mrs. Poulteney. Three chapters later, the narrator himself enlarges upon the vicar's story, making corrections and emendations wherever applicable. It is noteworthy that Sarah's biography develops by rumor and gossip, and that the narrator, even though he corrects it, fails also to relate the whole truth. Other revelations will follow, but, as the essence of Sarah is mystery, the whole truth cannot be told. No one but an omniscient god is qualified to tell it, and no such being exists in *The French Lieutenant's Woman.*

Sarah is also an only daughter, not of a wealthy merchant, but rather of a tenant-farmer of very modest means. Her father was obsessed with the gentility of his distant paternal ancestry, and it is because of this that she was sent to boarding school and educated beyond the station into which she was born. Not too long after her return from school at the age of eighteen, her father went mad from the combined pressures of his increased pecuniary difficulties and the need he felt to maintain his facade of gentility. He died in Dorchester Asylum, leaving his daughter—like Charles now—an orphan.

In her mid-twenties, with neither family nor social connections, Sarah was utterly alone and seemed destined to remain so. Her gift is also her cross: a rare and profound insight into human feeling, enabling her to establish strong bonds of sympathy with others, but also to see through their pretensions to what they really are. Her education conspires with her intelligence to produce the pariah. She has been given the trappings of a lady without the social standing; she has been forced out of her own class without being raised to the next. If there is a key to her actions, it lies in the combination of these seemingly determining circumstances and what she does to break the mold they have cast for her.

Upon the death of her father, she took the post of governess to Captain John Talbot's family at Charmouth, and proved a skillful teacher and beloved companion. It was here that she was allured by the apparently considerable charms of Lieutenant Varguennes, the injured French ship's officer, shipwrecked off the coast and nursed back to health by the governess, the only member of the household with a knowledge of French. After his recovery, Sarah unwisely followed him to Weymouth, only to be deserted shortly thereafter.

The events leading to Charles and Sarah's second meeting are plotted slowly and methodically, suggesting, as elsewhere, the slower pace of mid-Victorian rural life, and highlighting by contrast the sudden, spectacular moment of their confrontation. It is a rare and magnificent Dorset spring day, a "ravishing fragment of Mediterranean warmth and luminosity" when "nature goes a little mad." Ernestina, suffering from

her periodic indisposition, is unwilling to inflict its
consequences upon her fiancé. So Charles not unagree-
ably finds himself with a few solitary hours in which
to pursue his specialist interest in echinoderm, or petri-
fied sea urchin, found along the Dorset coast. Unaware
of the passage of time and the changing tides, Charles,
after several hours, must return by an inland route
and finds himself walking through the wild, unspoiled,
and desolate area known as the Undercliff near the sea
and Ware Commons inland. Its lush and exotic flora
are described with a naturalist's precision; its mysteries
and its dangers are evoked in sharp contrast to the
tame, civilized picture of the town.

As he is gradually finding his way out of this
"English Garden of Eden," he stumbles upon what at
first he takes to be a corpse, but upon inspection
realizes is the very much alive body of Sarah Woodruff, "in the complete abandonment of deep sleep."
Stunned, unable to do anything but stare down at the
motionless body, Charles is struck by her tenderness,
sure of her innocence, but also susceptible to her
evident sexuality and her "appalling" loneliness. "He
could not imagine what, besides despair, could drive
her, in an age where women were semistatic, timid,
incapable of sustained physical effort, to this wild
place." Suddenly, dramatically, she awakens, scram-
bles to her feet, and fixes her eyes upon him in shock
and amazement. He murmurs an embarrassed apology,
turns, and walks rapidly in the direction of Lyme.

The identification of this fertile and primitive area
with Eden, the discovery of the innocent yet sexual
woman, the intuition (for the second time) that the
woman is not of her time and is more in harmony with
wild nature than with Lyme Regis—all of this suggests the powerful, primal effect of the encounter. It
is a shock, a jolting awakening of long-repressed emotions, which, in a sense, provides the psychological

counterpart to the mythic Temptation and Fall. Indeed, the scene ends with the following: "Charles did not know it, but in those brief poised seconds above the waiting sea, in that luminous evening silence broken only by the waves' quiet wash, the whole Victorian Age was lost." As already mentioned, Charles's personal crisis will come to reflect that of the age, his personal awakening here equated with the end of an historical era. (It should also be noted that this primal scene symbolism recurs during their last meeting in the Undercliff, substantiating the above interpretation. At that time, the wood is described in religious terms, and Charles's communion with its vital spirit is called a "natural eucharist." However, by this time, there is the bitterness of alienation in the experience. Charles, while "stand[ing] here in Eden," feeling "in all ways excommunicated," "all paradise lost," is able to identify with Sarah the outcast.)

They meet about a week later, also by chance, this time face to face on a narrow path in the Undercliff. Charles is again transfixed by her face in which all has been "sacrificed" to the large, dark-brown eyes so evidently conveying her self-awareness, her fierce independence," "a determination to be what she was." The "suppressed intensity of her eyes" is "matched by the suppressed sensuality of her mouth." Again Charles feels "both repelled and lanced." Her features, we are reminded once more, are not those currently in fashion: specifically, the eyebrows are unusually dark and strong for an age favoring the fragile arched effect, and the mouth is wide in an age which cultivated the small, almost lipless standard. Though never specifically mentioned, it is by now clear to anyone who has seen the paintings of Dante Gabriel Rossetti, or his colleagues and disciples, that this enigmatic and melancholy beauty so suggestive of the passionate and suffering soul, those large eyes and bold features, and the ample, thick, loosened auburn hair are modelled after the ideal of feminine beauty which arose with the founding in 1848 of the defiant but very influential Pre-Raphaelite Brotherhood.[8] In this light as well, Sarah is ahead of her time, and it is not fortuitous that Fowles depicts her in an association with the Pre-Raphaelites at the close of the novel.

Another encounter follows soon afterward, on Ware Commons, when Charles finds his time freed for collecting by Ernestina's very convenient migraine attack (she *is* a delicate creature). On this occasion, however, it seems that Sarah has deliberately followed him. She appears above him, aglow, as it were, in an oblique shaft of sunlight, reminding Charles of an account he had heard of an epiphany of the Virgin Mary. She holds out two echinoderm specimens which he takes from her ungloved hand, their fingers momentarily touching. She says that she must unburden herself to him. After she drops to her knees and pleads, he consents to meet privately with her once more.

Fowles is at his best in describing these encounters, establishing the perfect natural setting to complement the human drama. The subtlety of the innuendo and ever-present irony, the evocation of strong though muted feelings, the formality of language and manner which hides (or partially hides) the suppressed sexual passions are all a tribute to the deftness of his touch and his sympathy with the age. There is a slow and deliberate building of tension, titillating suggestions of important omissions, and a thoroughly delicious promise of much more to come.

His contact with Sarah takes its toll in Charles's reflections upon his fiancée. By contrast with the melancholy sphinx, Ernestina is without depth of feeling, conditioned out of nearly all spontaneity. She is too limited for Charles, and, what is worse, she is capable of being wholly known. In contrast to Sarah's, her face becomes "a little characterless, a little monotonous." Sarah now symbolizes for Charles all the possibilities which will remain unrealized in marriage to Ernestina.

His rendezvous with Sarah is shortly accomplished, her "confession" constituting a more private and personal rendition of the previous accounts by Ernestina, the vicar, and the narrator. Like the vicar, Sarah lies about the crucial point: he told Mrs. Poulteney that she lodged with a female cousin at Weymouth; Sarah says that she slept with Varguennes. At this point we know the first to be a falsehood; the second remains our illusion until the climax of the novel. Sarah says that she gave herself to the French Lieutenant so that she "should never be the same again," because she knew no other way "to break out of what [she] was." She knows that she is not like other women and that they cannot understand her: "I have a freedom they cannot understand. No insult, no blame, can touch me. Because I have set myself beyond the pale."

Although at the heart of this self-analysis is a lie, and although Charles is not yet ready to understand what Sarah means by a freedom beyond the pale, her account provides an important clue to the motivation and meaning of her actions. She has refused to submit to the conventional life alotted her by society. Instead, as Jeff Rackham observes, "in the best existential[ist] manner, [she] has created a new self by her own choice, an authentic self, one outside the recognition of decent people and freed from their petty morals and conventions." Her choice is even more radical than it at first appears because, "not only has her freedom not been forced upon her by circumstances, the circumstances themselves have been invented."[9]

Her confession achieves its intended effect as Charles is "swept hopelessly away from his safe anchorage of judicial and judicious sympathy." He conjures up in his mind a fantastic scenario, in which she gives herself to the French Lieutenant and he (Charles) plays at one and the same time the roles of the seducer and the champion who comes forward to strike the villain down. "Deep in himself he forgave her her unchastity; and glimpsed the dark shadows where he might have enjoyed it himself." Sarah deliberately presses her finger upon a hawthorn branch, drawing the blood suggestive of her passion (in both senses) and the sexual act Charles has just imagined, as well as foreshadowing the climactic moment of their romance.

This scene of heightened emotions concludes with its comic counterpart. Upon returning to Lyme, they discover Charles's servant Sam and Mrs. Tranter's Mary making love in the same wood—playful, physical love, that is, something quite different from the repressive and frustrating business of the master. The comic love life below stairs is, in many ways, designed parallel to, and as comment upon, the love triangle on which we have been focusing. Until Charles's irremediable attachment to this *femme fatale,* Sam's destiny is linked with his master's (much like that of his namesake, Dickens's Sam Weller). Charles's ill-fortune, at least partially caused by Sam, will provide the ground from which Sam will begin his own transformation, his upward social climb.

Sarah is dismissed from Mrs. Poulteney's household. She writes to Charles imploring him to see her once more. However, before their final tryst in Lyme, this sequence is suspended for considerable time while Charles is informed that his uncle is engaged to be married to a much younger woman, and that Charles is liable to lose his substantial inheritance if an heir results from their union. Deeply troubled by Sarah, Charles seeks the advice of the humane and enlight-

ened Dr. Grogan (a particularized version of the stock
literary figure of the country doctor). Grogan's learned,
though obviously inadequate, opinion is that Sarah
Woodruff is what we should call today a hysteric. His
theory is amply supported by the fascinating and
authentic nineteenth-century case histories of melan-
cholia and sexual repression that the doctor gives
Charles to read. Grogan shocks his young friend by
telling him the already obvious fact that he is "half in
love with her," then counsels Charles to flee the temptress while he is still able.

Charles is now truly obsessed with Sarah. They
meet, for what Charles anticipates will be the last
time, in a secluded barn in the Undercliff. The rendezvous moves rapidly to the bursting of their pent-up
emotions:

He slowly reached out his hands and raised her [from her
knees]. Their eyes remained on each other's, as if they were
both hypnotized. She seemed to him—or those wide, those
drowning eyes seemed—the most ravishingly beautiful he
had ever seen. What lay behind them did not matter. The
moment overcame the age.

He took her into his arms, saw her eyes close as she
swayed into his embrace; then closed his own and found
her lips. He felt not only their softness but the whole close
substance of her body; her sudden smallness, fragility,
weakness, tenderness . . . .

He pushed her violently away.

. . . Then he turned and rushed through the door—
into yet another horror.

They are discovered by their more earthy counterparts,
Sam and Mary, who have also come to the barn, for
what, as our author-narrator says, "one can only
speculate."

Charles aids Sarah in her hasty departure from
Lyme. He provides her with money and sends her
belongings ahead of her to Exeter. The locale then

switches to London, where Charles has an interview with Mr. Freeman, during which the older man offers his intended son-in-law a partnership in his business. It is here that Charles must finally acknowledge the unbridgeable social gulf between them. Charles knows that, although the gentleman is a dying breed ("a superseded monster," a "poor living fossil"), he could never go into commerce, where the pursuit of money becomes the purpose of life. Yet he also realizes that his present lifestyle is entirely dependent upon having large sums of money and that Mr. Freeman may well be his primary source of wealth.

He takes refuge from his troubled thoughts in milk punch and champagne, a specialty of his London club. Charles adds claret and then port to what he has already consumed, becomes thoroughly intoxicated, and joins his companions in an exotic sexual escapade at the house of Ma Terpsichore. Before accomplishing what he apparently came for, Charles leaves the brothel in disgust, but then picks up a street prostitute who very faintly reminds him of the French Lieutenant's Woman. She too has been abandoned by a soldier-lover, but in her case there is a young daughter, with whom Charles has a brief scene foreshadowing the last of the story. Charles foolishly drinks some cheap hock which she offers him. Though sexually excited, the quantity and variety of alcohol he has consumed, in combination with the faint taste of onions in her mouth (Fowles omits no detail), proves, alas, too much for our hero. When the naked woman reveals that her name is Sarah, Charles, "racked by an intolerable spasm," begins vomitting upon the pillow beside her head. This brings to a sudden conclusion his night's debauche.

Returning to Lyme, his train must stop in Exeter. Charles has received a note from Sarah, only three words indicating her address, "Endicott's Family

Hotel," but he decides to take a carriage straight on to Lyme. To ignore the implicit invitation, to renew his faithfulness and his chastity, to return to his duty, his sacred vows of betrothal, all of these are encompassed by the decision of our Victorian hero. His destiny at this moment seems to him inexorably fixed. Sarah has become "the symbol around which had accreted all his lost possibilities, his extinct freedoms, his never-to-be-taken journeys." Whereas, in the evolutionary imagery reiterated throughout the novel, Charles used to think of himself as "naturally selected," belonging "undoubtedly to the fittest," he now sees himself as "one of life's victims, one more ammonite caught in the vast movements of history, . . . a potential turned to a fossil."[10]

"And so," we are audaciously informed one hundred pages from the close of the novel, "ends the story." Sarah's fate remains unknown. Charles and Ernestina marry and have seven children. Uncle Robert sires not one heir but twins. Charles enters Mr. Freeman's business.

This is the first of three endings to the story. While it does offer an alternative for Charles, it is quite obviously undercut by the abruptness with which it comes, the irony and insincerity with which it is related, and its humorous and heavy-handed impression of spontaneous fabrication ("they begat what shall it be—let us say seven children"; "who can be bothered with the biography of servants?"). While it is perhaps an alternative for the Victorian hero, it provides none at all for the modern. It is psychologically unconvincing, a betrayal of all that the novel has been moving towards. It has little air of reality about it, and is, indeed, offered as the purely conventional, the literary, ending. It is not surprising, therefore, that in the same chapter, Mrs. Poulteney, an entirely conventional figure, gets most of the attention, being given a justly vindictive after-life described at some length and with great fun. The novel form, Fowles tells us elsewhere, is "fundamentally a kind of game, an artifice that allows the writer to play hide-and-seek with the reader."[11] In *The French Lieutenant's Woman*, as in *The Magus*, Fowles plays with gusto.

The next chapter explains what the reader has already guessed, that the preceding was not what happened, but what Charles spent the journey from London to Exeter imagining *might* happen, his own autobiographical novel, so to speak. What "actually" happened was that the three-word missive from Sarah haunted him. Instead of feeling the end of his possibilities, dwelling upon her note facilitates the lucid recognition that he is entirely free to choose, that he can now shape his own destiny for himself. He decides to stay the night in Exeter and visits Endicott's Family Hotel. He hears that Sarah has twisted her ankle from a fall she took on the stairs. He must go up to her room if he wants to see her. Here the pace quickens, leading rapidly to the explosive climax of the novel. This moment of overwhelming passion is also the climax to "a long frustration—not merely sexual, for a whole ungovernable torrent of things banned, romance, adventure, sin, madness, animality." "All these coursed wildly through him" as he strained her body to his. Precisely ninety seconds later his passion is abated.

And then comes the shock: in "apocalyptic horror" he realizes from his blood-stained shirt tails that Sarah was a virgin, that she had not given herself to Varguennes. A moment later he sees that she walks without a limp, that there is no strained ankle. She has deliberately deceived him in order to ensnare him. The entire scene has been set, the whole passionate drama imagined by her beforehand. But why? "A swarm of mysteries."

He manages to rationalize Sarah's stratagems as
devices to "unblind him," to bring him to the full
realization of a "new vision" of personal freedom.
From this point until the final scene, the events occur
with celerity.

Charles sends Sarah a letter and a brooch via
Sam, but the servant turns traitor and neither are
delivered. Charles travels to Lyme to break his engage-
ment with Ernestina (he tells her what Sarah had
previously told him: "I am not worthy of you"). Sam
leaves his master's employ. His sad but necessary business in Lyme accomplished, Charles departs for Exeter
with another scenario in mind. This too turns out to be
pure fantasy: He and Sarah will go abroad; though
exiles, they will provide mutual consolation—"in some
jasmine-scented room they would lie awake, in each
other's arms, infinitely alone, exiled, yet fused in that
loneliness, inseparable in that exile." He is quickly
disillusioned in Exeter, where he discovers the servant's treachery and is informed that Sarah has departed
for London. Mr. Freeman forces Charles to sign a
confessio delicti, an admission of his guilt in the breaking of his solemn contract with Ernestina. After a
protracted but futile search for Sarah's whereabouts,
Charles decides to go abroad.

Reminiscent of the "waiting game" that forms the
last part of *The Magus*, though here of twenty months
duration, Charles, like Nicholas, has the opportunity
in this period to re-evaluate his experience. At the time
he had his vision of freedom, he was unaware of how
much that freedom depended on his fantasy of shared
exile. He must move towards a more mature and
realistic notion of freedom.

Finally, in New Orleans, the telegram arrives from
his solicitor: "She is found." Their reunion occurs at
16 Cheyne Walk, Chelsea. When Charles knocks on
the door, he has no idea that this is the once-infamous,

now-famous Rossetti household. He is ushered in by a young woman who he thinks is a maid, but quickly realizes is not. He expects to find Sarah employed as a governess, not as the artist's assistant and sometime model. The chapter masterfully traces first Charles's shock as, detail by detail, he becomes cognizant of the environment he has entered; then his further disillusionment as he realizes that the sibyl, even now, will not conform to his stereotyped fantasies, nor to others' definitions and delimitations of her. Charles is described as "a man woken into, not out of, a nightmare" and "as shaken as a man who suddenly finds the world around him standing on its head." The Sarah he meets is an "electric and bohemian apparition," dressed "in the uniform of the New Woman, flagrantly rejecting all formal contemporary notions of female fashion."

While the account of their interview is, as usual, rendered from Charles's point of view, this is the first time we are privy to Sarah's perspective on their relationship. She tells him there was "a madness" in her at the time, there was "a falsehood" in their relationship from the beginning. Her past has habituated her to loneliness and she values her loneliness more than she had previously imagined. She is genuinely happy in Rossetti's house, in the society of genius from which she has much to gain and to which she can contribute in humble ways. In short, she does not wish to share her life. Echoing an earlier perception of Charles's, she says, "I wish to be what I am, not what a husband, however kind, however indulgent, must expect me to become in marriage."

Charles analyzes the situation differently. He feels that he has been victimized and that she exults in his despair. He turns to leave, but Sarah will not let him go under such an illusion. She reveals to him "what a less honorable gentleman might have guessed," that

a daughter has resulted from their brief sexual encounter. The final moment of this protracted scene, the
long-wished-for moment (by Charles and, I dare say,
most readers as well) of the re-affirmation of love, is,
unfortunately, too sentimental for the author of *The
Collector* and *The Magus,* too pat, too simple. There
is a sudden turning towards a providential God,
which rings true for neither Fowles nor his agnostic
creation:

And he comprehended: it had been in God's hands, in His
forgiveness of their sins. Yet still he stared down at her
hidden face. . . .

At last she looked up at him. Her eyes were full of
tears, and her look unbearably naked. Such looks we have
all once or twice in our lives received and shared; they are
those in which worlds melt, pasts dissolve, moments when
we know, in the resolution of profoundest need, that the
rock of ages can never be anything else but love, here,
now, in these two hands' joining, in this blind silence in
which one head comes to rest beneath the other; and
which Charles, after a compressed eternity, breaks, though
the question is more breathed than spoken.

"Shall I ever understand your parables?"

The head against his breast shakes with a mute vehe-
mence. A long moment. The pressure of lips upon auburn
hair.

The critical reader must remain skeptical, disappointed by the artificiality of the scene, by the feeling
that Charles has not taken his "journey" to its end,
that this cannot be the end. Fowles is, of course,
mainly exercising his imagination—and gleefully toy-
ing with the reader's emotions. There is another
chapter in which we return to Charles's accusations
of the previous scene: "You have not only planted the
dagger in my breast, you have delighted in twisting it."
He turns on his heels, moves toward the door. She
detains him. To his shock, there is the suggestion of a

smile "in her eyes, if not about her lips." Then the revelation of the alternate ending comes upon him:

He sought her eyes for some evidence of her real intentions, and found only a spirit prepared to sacrifice everything but itself—ready to surrender truth, feeling, perhaps even all womanly modesty in order to save its own integrity. . . . He saw his own true superiority to her: which was not of birth or education, not of intelligence, not of sex, but of an ability to give that was also an ability to compromise. She could give only to possess; and to possess him . . . was not enough.

As with *The Collector* and *The Magus,* Fowles has titled his novel after the character manifesting the most power in it. Sarah is as much the mover of the action here as Clegg is in *The Collector* and Conchis in *The Magus.* In these terms, Sarah—with her powerful, dominant will and her need to possess on the one hand, and, on the other, her uniqueness, her insight, her personal magnetism, and her distinct flair for the dramatic—is a composite figure in the Fowles corpus, part Magus and part Collector. No less than Astarte, the goddess to whom Fowles dedicated *The Magus,* Sarah Woodruff is his tribute to the mystery of woman, mystery meant in the sense of the second epigraph heading this chapter.

Sarah is, then, essentially unfathomable. "Who is Sarah? Out of what shadows does she come?" asks the author-narrator early in the story. His answer: "I do not know." She herself tells Charles: "I am not to be understood even by myself. And I can't tell you why, but I believe my happiness depends on my not understanding." We, like Charles, must be content to observe this figure and to admit in the end that we cannot fathom her depths, that perhaps the epithets "oxymoron," "Sphinx," "enigma," "Delphic," which appear throughout, are as accurate as we and the author can be.

Charles flees the room. Descending the stairs, he sees the woman who greeted him at the door, this time holding a child in her arms, a child whose identity is not clarified in this ending. As Charles walks through the gate of the Rossetti house, he is in a sense "reborn." Life lies before him, his path undetermined. He has found at last "an atom of faith in himself, a true uniqueness, on which to build."

He must create himself as Sarah has done before him. She provides Charles with an insight similar to that which Conchis gives Nicholas. In the end, the power of Sarah as well as Conchis lies not in what they preach, but what they do. Or rather what they *are,* for it is the shock of the human encounter itself that carries the transforming power. Charles has already begun to realize "that life, however advantageously Sarah may in some ways seem to fit the role of Sphinx, is not a symbol, is not one riddle and one failure to guess it, is not to inhabit one face alone or to be given up after one losing throw of the dice; but is to be, however inadequately, emptily, hopelessly into the city's iron heart, endured."

The other ending, the traditional romantic one, is wish-fulfillment. The neatness of its resolution is unacceptable in an age in which lucid and simple resolutions are so few and far between. This one, unreconciled and open-ended—again like *The Magus*— is truer to contemporary experience. *The French Lieutenant's Woman* ends with the final line from Matthew Arnold's "To Marguerite." This is the poem which we were earlier told Charles had "committed to heart" (by which, I take it, is meant something more than memory), and which he and his author-narrator agree is "the noblest short poem of the whole Victorian era." The poem's dominant metaphor compares humanity to so many islands in the sea of life, between them ordained always and forever "the unplumb'd, salt, estranging sea."

The seemingly experimental device of multiple endings was not unknown to Victorian novelists.[12] In combination with the ambiguous narrative voice and the tenuous fictional illusion, it becomes a means of suggesting that the inventive contemporary novelist can write an experimental novel and still remain identifiably within the great tradition of the English novel. I have traced the main subject of *The French Lieutenant's Woman* in the fictional history of Charles and Sarah. Another significant, though perhaps less obvious, subject of *The French Lieutenant's Woman* is the contemporary novel itself, or rather the difficult task of writing a contemporary novel.

"The situation of the novelist today," writes David Lodge, "may be compared to a man standing at a crossroads. The road on which he stands . . . is the realistic novel, the compromise between fictional and empirical modes."[13] This is the dominant tradition of the English novel to date, the tradition in which Fowles very definitely sees himself. The paths branching off at the crossroads, according to Lodge, lead, in one direction, to the so-called "non-fiction novel" made popular by Truman Capote and Norman Mailer; and, in the other direction, to the purely fictional modes of myth, allegory, and romance. The choice of roads is today's dilemma. In regard to contemporary fiction, Fowles's achievement in *The French Lieutenant's Woman* is to have re-established the novelist's path, while simultaneously modifying his stride and augmenting his provisions.

The Ebony Tower

Just as many priests became so pre-occupied
with ritual and the presentation of doctrine that
they forgot the true nature of the priesthood, so
have many artists become so blind to all but the
requirements of style that they have lost all
sight of, or pay no more than lip service to,
any human moral content.—*The Aristos*[1]

. . . he felt that the augury he had sought in the
wheeling darting birds and in the pale space of
sky above him had come forth from his heart
like a bird from a turret quietly and swiftly.
Symbol of departure or loneliness?—James Joyce,
Portrait of the Artist as a Young Man

The Ebony Tower consists of four original stories and
a modern prose rendering of a twelfth-century French
love story, Marie de France's *Eliduc*. The collection
affords us our first experience of Fowles working in
the shorter fictional forms. The stories within stories
of *The Magus* and *The French Lieutenant's Woman*
bespoke Fowles's promise as a short story writer. They
already demonstrated his capacity for rapid portraiture, immediate evocation of mood and atmosphere,
and brief but striking narrative effects. Although similar in many ways to his novels, the subjects for the
stories in this collection apparently came to him quite

suddenly. Interrupting the writing of *Daniel Martin,* he turned out the first drafts of all of them in just a few days.[2]

In a personal note preceding Fowles's "Eliduc," the author explains that the working title he used for the volume was "Variations." By this he intended to suggest "variations both on certain themes in previous books of [his] and in methods of narrative presentation." The title was eventually discarded because of the judgment of his publisher that the title was without justification except as "a very private mirage in the writer's mind." Fowles mentions this, no doubt, because he still believes the working title was appropriate, a belief with which I would wholeheartedly concur.

To begin with, *The Ebony Tower* breaks very little new ground in terms of thought or subject. The themes, characters, and imagery of the title story of the collection are very close to those of *The Magus.* The concerns that unify all five of these tales are the same that unify the corpus as a whole: matters of love and sex, the functions of art and the artist, the uses and abuses of language, the demands of freedom and the responsibilities of free choice, and so on. The careful reader who is acquainted with Fowles's previous fiction will certainly note the correspondence between this collection of stories and the other works. In fact, a familiarity with the previous fiction adds another dimension to one's understanding and enjoyment of these stories.

The reason that Fowles's personal note appears as the headnote to "Eliduc" is that *The Ebony Tower* "is also a variation of a more straightforward kind," namely, of the influence of the twelfth-century romance, and more specifically of the tales of Marie de France. His book, he claims, owes its "mood" and much of its "theme and setting" to her work. The courtly love stress on "keeping faith," especially in sexual relations, which is central to "Eliduc," is an important specific theme running through Fowles's novels and the stories of *The Ebony Tower*. Furthermore, the stories and the novels contain variations on the motif of the ordeal so characteristic of the medieval romance. Like the medieval knight errant, each of Fowles's protagonists can be seen to undergo a kind of ordeal at a crucial point in his or her life. The experience upsets the character's equilibrium, thereby altering his self-image and the direction in which he hitherto thought his life had been heading.

"Variations" is an equally apt description of Fowles's methods of narrative presentation. With *The Ebony Tower*, he emerges as a writer's writer. Each of his stories is a virtuoso piece. Each transforms the expected and conventional into something unexpected and unconventional. Remarking on the complexity and power of the four original stories, one reviewer says: "it's as though one had picked up a simple, familiar object, casually examined it and suddenly found it shaking in one's hands."[3] Each of the pieces affords its author a special challenge, and watching him meet that challenge provides much of the interest of the reading experience.

The stories also hold unusual problems for the critic. Their meaning is generally elusive, not at all easy to articulate. The action is usually minimized. Reminiscent in some ways of a Chekov play, say *The Seagull* or *The Cherry Orchard*, the action of these tales seems "internal" rather than external. They are built less upon the overt actions of the characters than upon the characters' internal or private reactions. Promised climaxes and revelations do not often materialize. Conclusions remain provocative and frustrating, leaving the reader begging for another line or two, another clue to the mystery of the tales.

❖   ❖   ❖

The first and title piece is the most substantial of the collection. "The Ebony Tower" is probably best described as a novella, a form intermediate in length and complexity between a short story and a full-length novel. Even here, however, very little actually happens. The central character suffers a sense of loss and failure, experiencing the "eternally missed chance." As this phrase implies, the story turns not on what he does, but on what he fails to do or cannot do.

David Williams, lecturer, art critic, and artist of some renown, is writing the biographical and critical introduction to a book devoted to the work of the old and famous expatriot painter Henry Breasley. To this end, he comes for a weekend, in the late summer of 1973, to the seventy-seven year old artist's Breton farm house for a rare interview with the "life long exile." The story is heavily dependent on the atmosphere of the *manoir* and its secluded forest setting, both described in detail. Henry Breasley shares his huge house with an elderly gardener, a housekeeper (his one-time model), and two sexually provocative young women. One of them, a former student at the Royal College of Art, is his very talented amanuensis named Diana. Henry has re-christened her "the Mouse" by combining the word "Muse" with the picture of an O-shaped vulva, thus uniting in the nickname her two primary functions in the household. The other woman is Anne, called "the Freak," also a former art student, though not as promising or serious as Diana. Both of these nubile and frequently naked companions tend to the ageing artist's professional and personal needs, the latter amounting mainly to a kind of "nursing" and to servicing his greatly diminished but still evident sexual appetite.

Breasley and Williams are both artistic types and realistically drawn individuals. The contrast of the two men contributes to the theme, already well-established in *The Collector* and *The Aristos,* of the nature of the true artist and his function in the modern world. The young man, thirty-one years of age, is successful and affable, "above all tolerant, fair-minded and inquisitive." Though a contemporary artist of great promise, the felt need for more money combined with a "small personal crisis of doubt about his own work" have led David into lecturing and reviewing. His painting is fully abstract, or entirely nonrepresentational, and, in the 1960s, was associated with the Op Art Movement. Although of a high technical standard, David knows that the main reason his paintings have sold so well is their pleasant decorative appeal.

"The Ebony Tower" contains a critique of contemporary art, as well as the society which produces it and which it reflects. Like Nicholas Urfe, David is meant to be a representative of the age. In his brief life can be seen the reflection of the failures of the age, or what Fowles considers to be its failures. Like Nicholas, David's first impulse is disengagement and avoidance. He lacks the passion, the drive, and the inner direction of the true artist. It is ultimately the "fear of challenge" that governs his life and his work: "One killed all risk, one refused all challenge, and so one became an artificial man." He tries to conceal his life in the craft of his art. His art, in fact, is nothing but craft.

Henry's life, on the other hand, has always consisted of the quest for challenge. Henry is entirely self-centered, fiercely opinionated, "profoundly amoral." He is called the "great man," but also the "old devil," the "wicked old faun," the "frightful old bastard." He is a modern-day pagan, with none of the younger man's urbanity and grace.

The Mouse remarks rather tamely, but very significantly, that Henry "thinks one shouldn't show toleration for things one believes are bad." What is perceived as intolerance is, in effect, Henry's commitment. David seems committed to nothing and so he is extremely tolerant, by definition as it were. The old artist has the passion, the single-mindedness, and the courage to be what he is entirely. He has honesty and integrity. His strength as an artist lies in "not letting anything stand between self and expression," which is not simply a matter of style or technique, but of "how you did it," "how wholly, how bravely you faced up to the constant recasting of yourself." "Just paint," is the artist's advice. "Leave the clever talk to the poor sods who can't."

Henry is unequivocal in his disdain for abstract art. He sees it as the betrayal of all that art is or should be, as "a flight from human and social responsibility." Its cerebral, mechanical, purely conventional qualities represent what he calls the "triumph of the bloody eunuch." Abstraction belies the fear of, and consequent lack of contact with, the human body. It conceals the artist instead of exposing him. Henry's term for what he dislikes in contemporary art, for the obscurity he thinks arises from the artist's fear of being clear and being known, is the "ebony tower."

There are two strands to the plot, each of which presents a type of ordeal for David, thus forcing comparison with the plots of medieval romance—at least with *Eliduc* and Chretien de Troyes's *Yvain,* from which the epigraph to "The Ebony Tower" is taken. David may be seen as the ironic, even pathetic, modern counterpart of the medieval knight errant, a figure alluded to more than once in the novella. Each strand, in its own way, also deals with the fear of the body and of exposing the real self. The dominant one centers upon David's growing familiarity with Breasley and develops the ideas on modern art and modern life style outlined above. Its high point occurs after dinner on the first evening, when the old man delivers a drunken tirade on the "ebony tower." David holds up remarkably well under Henry's assault, described variously as David's "baptism of fire," as a "test," "ordeal," and "buffeting."

David "sailed past that preposterously obvious reef" only to be challenged again at "the real rock of truth," in the rapidly evolving relationship with Diana that forms the second strand of the plot. David at first is understandably ill at ease amidst the kinky *ménage à trois* formed by the old artist and his girls. The mutual attraction of David and Diana, however, increases during the next day's picnic, a strange and provocative affair evoking Manet's *Déjeuner sur L'herbe*. At the picnic, David feels, or is made to feel, that he must "prove himself" to the girls, and he "establishes his credentials" with a shared swim in the nude. The personal and social concerns in the old man's critique of modernism are plainly exemplified in the failed love encounter that evening of these two thoroughly modern young people.

Like his medieval predecessor, Eliduc, David is married to a loving and faithful wife. He is torn between his duty to her and his desire for the other.[4] The scene is an already familiar one in Fowles's *oeuvre*, erotic but unconsummated. The act of sex, as Peter Prince has noted, is entirely absent from the story. "It is all watching and wishing and dreaming, and the brilliant manipulation of such quite commonplace stimuli as female nudity and feminine subservience before male demands."[5] Diana ultimately rejects him, though her motive is less than crystal clear. Perhaps it is David's hesitation, perhaps her realization that the relationship would never grow into anything more, or perhaps—as Lorna Sage suggests—it is a matter of their "wanting each other in successive moments, coming achingly close, but never coinciding."[6]

The scene provides the climax, or anti-climax, of

the novella, following which is a weighty (perhaps too weighty for the situation) scene of recognition and self-analysis. Emerging quite clearly is David's sense of loss and failure: "He had failed both in the contemporary and the medieval sense; as someone who wanted sex, as someone who renounced it." The dynamic power of Breasley finally and fully impresses itself upon him. At first the old artist is merely an object of curiosity, a subject for an essay. The weekend encounter, however, proves traumatic for the young man. His life and his art have been harshly tested. Both unfortunately attest to the "jettisoning of the human body and its natural physical perceptions." This is the principal message of the story.

In the tale of another author, such trauma would be seen to produce a radical transformation in outlook or behavior. In Fowles's story, however, we are left with the impression of impotence. As he was unable to follow the promptings of the flesh, so he is unable now to act upon his insights. Driving away from the enchanted forest, toward the plane that will take him back to his wife and family, David ultimately realizes that nothing will change him or his painting:

he would go on painting as before, he would forget this day, he would find reasons to interpret everything differently. . . . He was crippled by common sense, he had no ultimate belief in chance and its exploitation, the missed opportunity would become the finally sensible decision, the decent thing: the flame of deep fire that had singed him a dream, a moment's illusion; her reality just one more unpursued idea. . . .

The Magus and The French Lieutenant's Woman end with their protagonists' awareness of expanded horizons and new directions because they stress the translation of important perceptions into freely chosen acts. The point here seems to be that without action,

the insights are lost and the transformation of personality not possible.

The next original story in the collection, "Poor
Koko," shares with "The Ebony Tower" the theme of
the unlived life. The anonymous first-person narrator
is a man who has spent his life in retreat from life,
with books, "writing them, reading, reviewing, helping
to get them into print." They have been his "life rather
more than life itself." He has passed an urbane and
very safe sixty-six years in London, fearing and de-
testing violence, even most forms of physical contact.
Always a puny man, he has, in self-defense, developed
a compensatory cerebral wit. He is very near to com-
pleting a lifetime ambition, the definitive biographical
and critical study of Thomas Love Peacock (incidentally one of Fowles's favorite nineteenth-century
writers).

Our narrator suddenly, and for the first time in his
life, has the knowledge (and accompanying anxiety)
that he is "not alone in a house where [he] believed
[he] was." The house, far from the London he knows
so well, is the deserted Holly Cottage, in a remote
area of north Dorset, a place borrowed from friends
as a retreat in which to finish the book.

His fears materialize in the shape of a young,
stocking-masked, kitchen-gloved burglar, to whom he
submits immediately and entirely. Like the two artists
of "The Ebony Tower," these unnamed antagonists,
while individualized, come also to represent antago-
nistic socio-political positions. In the narrator's mind,
the young bully belongs to the "new world of the
classless British young," those who rob the bourgeois
establishment as much from a sense of revolutionary
duty as for the money and goods to be acquired. In
their rejection of much that should be rejected of the
bourgeois life, he thinks, they have unfortunately also

discarded "respect for language and intellectual honesty" and the accompanying appreciation of some of the subtle complexities of sophisticated living. These, of course, form the basic components of the victim's daily life and ideals.

The at first inexplicable, the "bestial and totally gratuitous act of vandalism" that forms the climax to this slight tale is the silent, methodical burning of the author's manuscript and his irreplaceable documents. After this, as with "The Ebony Tower," there follows a brief reflective and analytic section concluding the story. At first the narrator shares his bewilderment over the meaning of, and motive for, the deed. Then he offers a tentative but attractive hypothesis. Their antagonism is interpreted as a clash of linguistic attitudes underlying the more obvious cultural ones. The man who lives by his pen reveres the power and magic of language. The other, who is not the master of its uses, deeply mistrusts that power. The destruction of the manuscript was, for the burglar, a symbolic victory in the war of cultural breakdown waged continually in the modern world.

As "The Ebony Tower" recalls *The Magus*, so "Poor Koko" takes us back to *The Collector*. The settings and situations of the two works are similar. Both depict an episode in the class conflict and both give the victory to the philistine. Miranda Grey in *The Collector* and the anonymous author in "Poor Koko" are too weak to fight their antagonists effectively. Their hatred of violence, even when necessary for self-defense, proves totally enfeebling in the circumstances in which they find themselves. Frederick Clegg and the hoodlum, on the other hand, share a fundamental suspicion and resentment of language and culture. *The Collector* is Fowles's least complex novel; "Poor Koko" is his simplest tale.

*   *   *

When John Marcus Fielding disappeared, he "contravened all social and statistical probability"—at least according to the data with which "The Enigma" commences. He was almost forty years out of his teens. He was not, and never had been, a vagabond. He had always seemed satisfied with his domestic life. He was not, nor ever had been, even close to being a member of the working class. On the contrary, John Marcus Fielding, was a highly successful, very wealthy London executive and Tory M.P. Hitherto he had proven entirely responsible and trustworthy in both public and private affairs. His disappearance, evidently without the aid of an accomplice, provides his wife and three children, his private secretary, his friends, and even the police force of Scotland Yard with a permanently baffling enigma.

As this curious story progresses from an entirely motiveless disappearance to an entirely clueless investigation, one wonders how Fowles could have made a story of it at all, let alone so absorbing and winning a one as this. Although we never meet the man, Fielding emerges in an intimate personality profile. This is compiled from the objective account of the narrator and from the investigation of the thoroughly unstereotyped Special Branch Sergeant, Michael Jennings, who emerges as the main actor in the story. The fullness of Fielding's portrait results from the variety of persons and points of view that are brought to bear on the man and his life: the wife, with her social and domestic role to maintain above all else; the adoring though somewhat shallow daughters; the rebellious son; the faithful spinster-secretary; Fielding's farm manager; his neighbors and professional associates; and last but far from least, Isobel Dodgson, his son's girlfriend. When Sergeant Jennings meets Miss Dodgson, the focus of "The Enigma" begins to shift from the problem of Fielding's disappearance to the mystery of love.

Isobel is one more lovely variation on the intelligent, sensitive, independent female who plays so active
and essential a role in the *dramatis personae* of the
Fowles canon. She is a highly imaginative, budding
young writer, with her own unusual and intuitive
theory of Fielding's disappearance. Her notion of
Fielding is that of a man severely limited, his thought
and behavior largely determined by the social system
in which he operates and with which he cooperates.
In the end, she says, he does what the system demands.
He can only play the various roles available to him,
the outlines and perhaps the details of which have
been clear from his assumption of the parts.

This is a case of life imitating art. The system, in
Isobel's metaphor, becomes the "author in his life."
Reminiscent of Nicholas's self-characterization, Isobel
says that Fielding is "like something written by some-
one else, a character in fiction. Everything is planned.
Mapped out."

Forgetting that she has committed Fielding to a
choiceless existence in a determined world—and incidentally illustrating a principal inconsistency of imaginative writers who are not also philosophers—
Isobel hypothesizes that his motive was to opt out
completely, without trace, without explanation. If any
clue to his whereabouts or any motive for his action
is discovered, then "he's back in a story, being written.
A nervous breakdown. A nut case. Whatever." This is
what she calls "God's trick," an image reminiscent of
the final move in the godgame of *The Magus*. Also
not dissimilar to the image of God in *The Aristos* and
The French Lieutenant's Woman, he is compared to
"the God who went missing," who walked out on his
creation. Fielding will gain a sort of immortality by
never being discovered: "The one thing people never
forget is the unsolved. Nothing lasts like a mystery."
Like *The Magus* again, the absconding god sparks the

fire of love in the young couple he has deserted. The story concludes with: "The tender pragmatisms of flesh have poetries no enigma, human or divine, can diminish or demean—indeed, it can only cause them, and then walk out."

"The Enigma" begins as a conventional mystery story, but concludes in the open-ended manner of the novels. A detective story without ending or solution, in which the central character makes no appearance, it is a *tour de force* of narrative craft. Indeed, Theodore Solotaroff interprets its primary subject as fictional narrative itself: "The underlying point of the story is that there is a wisdom that passes scientific understanding embedded in the narrative process itself, one that can weave intuition, imagination and reason into deep but lucid inquiries into human conduct and destiny."[7]

The final piece, "The Cloud," ends the way "The Enigma" begins, with a disappearance and possible suicide, this time that of the inscrutable Catherine. "The Cloud" seems to me Fowles's most difficult work to penetrate, certainly the most opaque in *The Ebony Tower*. Everything in this delicate mood piece is understated, muted, or ambiguous. Crucial expository information is withheld. Relationships of seemingly long-standing intimacy are only partially revealed. Tensions within and among the various characters remain unresolved, and are generally only partially exposed in any case. A sense of urgency persists unabated throughout the story, creating anxiety in the reader when its cause is not revealed. The feeling is intensified at the end, which is left threatening yet deliberately inaccessible. The whole reflects the psychic condition of Catherine: "so static . . . yet so potent and so poised."

The dominant effect of the story is incongruity

and disharmony, immediately established by the contrast of its title and its opening words: "a noble day,
young summer soaring, vivid with promise. . . ." The
eight characters clash with their setting: they are
urban Anglo-Saxons in the "so leafy, so liquid" natural
setting of central France. The opening pages are difficult and disorienting. The story-line, such as it is,
develops elliptically and dispassionately. At the same
time, it manages to be menacing. The characters call
each other by name before the reader has had time to
know who they are, and other elements of the dialogue
are deliberately obscured.

The whole is likened to a painted scene mysteri-
ously come alive:

The scene possessed a strange sense of enclosure, almost
that of a painting, a Courbet perhaps—or would have if
the modern clothes of the eight personages and their colors
had not clashed, in a way a totally urban and synthetic age
cannot be expected to notice, with the setting. . . . So many
things clashed, or were not what one might have expected.

As if in mist, however, many of the elements of this
picture remain indistinct. One never gets a long or
proper look at it. The perspectives seem to be constantly shifting as if its functions were the exploration
of various modes of perception.

Peter, his girlfriend Sally, and Tom, his son by his
deceased wife, have come to join Paul and Annabel,
their two daughters, and Annabel's sister Catherine
for a day's outing. Peter is a television producer and
Paul is a popular writer. Catherine has recently suffered a traumatic loss, apparently the death (perhaps
by suicide) of her husband. She is the "odd woman
out" in this otherwise gay and superficial group. She
"lies silent behind her dark glasses, like a lizard; sun-
ridden, storing, self-absorbed; much more like the day
than its people." She is unaffected by the clichés that

help ordinary, that is, less sensitive and more com-
promising, people to maintain their emotional balance
and their ability to carry on. She is a lost "island" in a
"limitless sea."

There is a complex life of feeling beneath the
surface of this picture, always pulsing, occasionally
correlated with a gesture or a word, but difficult to
articulate with precision. This is the soul of the piece,
evoked by words that hint at states of being for which
words are ultimately inadequate. The basic clash in
"The Cloud" is between the rippling surface illusions
and the dark and deep undercurrent of emotional
realities. If, as Fowles has reiterated in *The Aristos*
and elsewhere, existence is the tension of opposites,
then this short, delicately-fashioned piece, with its
uncharacteristic absence of didacticism, may consti-
tute a slice of life as he sees it.

By late afternoon the cloud has come, mysteri-
ously, ominously from the south, making the still
peaceful, sunny sky immediately overhead appear
"eerie, false, sardonic, the claws of a brilliantly dis-
guised trap." As we observe the subtle interactions of
the group, we come to realize that its relative calm and
gaiety is as sardonic as the trap which is the sky
overhead. It forms a false impression, at first unreveal-
ing of the emotional storm beneath the surface. The
gathering cloud is an epiphany in James Joyce's sense
of the immediate and potent spiritual manifestation
associated with an object or event, the significance of
which the observer suddenly apprehends. In this
connection, Fowles has remarked that he perceives in
"The Cloud" a feeling of "The Dead," the last story in
Joyce's early collection entitled *Dubliners*.[8]

Fowles says also that "The Cloud" was written as
"a deliberate homage to Katherine Mansfield."[9] Her
beauty, sensitivity, and talent, her lonely and suffering
existence, and her pathetically early death at age

thirty-four provided the basis for the Mansfield legend. It is easy to believe that her life inspired Fowles's creation of Catherine. The depression, the fragmentation of personality, the repulsion from the brutal and the commonplace—all are reminiscent of Katherine Mansfield. Fowles's story also suggests the influence of her work, as many of her short stories center upon the young, sensitive individual confronting a vapid and alien modern world.

Once again, Fowles has used a very slight story to achieve quite remarkable effects in a very brief span of time. The narrative techniques are especially impressive. At first, the entire group is presented within the natural setting. Then smaller groups are formed and isolated, mainly in pairs, such as husband and wife, sisters, father and son, aunt and niece, friends, and rivals. These relationships are conveyed largely through dialogue. Individuals are also isolated and rapidly characterized, this time mainly through interior monologue. The effect of these combined techniques is to provide the subtle but dynamic interplay of surface and depth, and of group and individual.

"The Cloud" unobtrusively and undidactically illuminates the difficulties and the different levels of human communication. It illustrates the devices one uses to isolate oneself, to enter into relationships with others, to avoid or to gain mastery over others. It lays bare and examines the conventions of social intercourse, particularly the relation of overt behavior to covert intention. It insists upon the essential isolation of each separate being, this idea reinforced by the recurrent image of isolated, disconnected, "islands" of human experience.

For those readers willing to work at it and able to appreciate it, "The Cloud" will provide a rare and rewarding experience. That it was placed at the end of the collection is perhaps indication of Fowles's awareness of his unique achievement.

The original pieces of *The Ebony Tower* do not seem, at first sight, to provide especially bountiful subjects for interesting stories. They are largely static, without much action, and without resolutions. Yet each, in its own way, is a stylistic gem, and each contains novel and fascinating perceptions. All fairly slight works by comparison with the long novels, they nevertheless attest to Fowles's mastery of a wide variety of narrative styles and his willingness to address himself to important ethical and social concerns.

Daniel Martin

> The one thing a modern writer should not be
> committed to: a style. The next great
> mega-European [i.e., Western] writer will write
> in all the styles, as Picasso has painted, and
> Stravinsky composed. This does not mean a
> loss of identity. The loss of identity occurs in the
> sacrifice of everything to the fear of loss of identity.
> —Fowles, "I Write Therefore I Am"[1]

Chosen as the epigraph to this concluding chapter is
an excerpt from a little-known piece published at the
beginning of the John Fowles's career. A kind of mani-
festo for the newly published author, it contains the
ideal with which this study commenced. Stylistic variety has been Fowles's aim from the start. It is his hall-
mark as a writer today. *Daniel Martin*, his most recent
novel, is yet another experiment in style. Although
many of Fowles's earlier preoccupations are quite evident in *Daniel Martin*, the novel nonetheless represents, in crucial ways, a significant departure from
his earlier fiction.

Daniel Martin is a well-known English dramatist
turned Hollywood scenarist and also novelist-to-be. He
shares with Fowles's previous protagonists the tendency to view himself as a scripted character of his
own creation: "I was writing myself, making myself

the chief character in a play, so that I was not only the written personage, the character and its actor, but also the person who sits in the back of the stalls admiring what he has written." Daniel interrupts his affair with Jenny McNeil, a young British film actress living in Los Angeles, to return home to England at the request of his old, though for many years estranged, Oxford friend, Anthony Mallory. Anthony's wife, Jane, is the woman Daniel should have married over twenty years ago; not her sister, Nell, whom he did. All four of them know this. Both marriages were false from the start: the Martins' ended years ago in divorce; the Mallorys' will end shortly with the shocking death of Anthony.

Anthony remained on at Oxford as a don. He is a practising Catholic and an academic philosopher, now in hospital with terminal cancer. He has asked to see Daniel before he dies in the hope of finally setting things right, or, in his words, "of correcting a design failure." He effects a reconciliation between himself and his old friend and then attempts to prepare Daniel for the ultimate reconciliation between him and Jane. Anthony's "hope against hope" is that Daniel will agree "to help disinter the person Jane might have been from beneath the person she now is." The sincerity of his plea and the seriousness of the task are dramatically emphasized by this life-long Catholic's suicide following the interview.

The reunion of the four begins a period of reminiscence, soul-searching, and re-evaluation for Daniel. He, too, feels severed from the person he might have been. He feels that he has betrayed his most distinctive qualities, namely, his ability to write and to love ("handling words, and loving one single other human being wholly").

Atonement for the first betrayal comes through the book *Daniel Martin,* understood to be the novel that Daniel has been planning but failing to write throughout his story. It is this novel that presumably indicates he has overcome his fear of exposing his true self. For him the novel represents an "exorcism by the written word." It is the realization of Daniel's "longing for a medium that would tally better with [the] real structure of [his] racial being and mind . . . something dense, interweaving, treating time as horizontal, like a skyline; not cramped, linear and progressive."

Atonement for the other betrayal comes from picking up the pieces of his past, restoring those in need of restoration, and building—through mature love and compassion—an authentic relationship with Jane. The final quarter of the novel documents the deliberate groping towards such a relationship. It culminates in the chapter entitled "The End of the World," set in the wasteland of Palmyra, Syria. Here, amidst the ruins of the dead city and the lifeless earth, their love is rejuvenated. The "design failure" is corrected through "disinterment" as Anthony had hoped it would be.

Like *The Magus* and *The French Lieutenant's Woman, Daniel Martin* is a large and difficult novel; unlike them, it sometimes makes for plodding, even ponderous reading. "A long journey of a book," is the way Fowles himself has characterized it in a recent radio interview.[2] Its composition was interrupted for the writing of *The Ebony Tower* and the rewriting of *The Magus.* Written leisurely, it was intended to be read in the same manner. With *Daniel Martin,* it is clear that Fowles has deliberately suspended his well-proven talent for telling suspenseful or thrilling tales. What is most prominent here is the expression of the novelist's freedom to digress from the story line, his capacity to fracture chronology, even to halt the passage of time altogether for excursions into tangential areas and times past. Whereas the digressions in

The Magus and *The French Lieutenant's Woman* always return us to a strong and fascinating narrative
.sequence, in *Daniel Martin* the return is simply to the
narrator himself.

This is Fowles's first novel whose title is the same
as the name of its hero, suggesting how thoroughly
the character's life is the subject of the book. Furthermore, in terms of thought and feeling, Fowles is
probably closer to Daniel Martin than to any of his
other protagonists. The frequent excursions into history, politics, natural history, film making, and many
other such diverse fields have the effect of creating a
fiction replete with fact, and a character who reveals
the author in fundamental ways. At a crucial point
about two-thirds through the book (at the end of the
chapter entitled "In the Orchard of the Blessed"),
Daniel gets the first glimpse of what he must do with
his novel. Nowhere is the blending of character and
author clearer or more significant than in the moral
and aesthetic declaration that follows this recognition:
"To hell with cultural fashion; to hell with elitist guilt;
to hell with existentialist nausea; and above all, to hell
with the imagined that does not say, not only in, but
behind the images, the real." Perhaps the most persua-
sive symbol of the reciprocity between character and
author in *Daniel Martin* is the proposed name of the
hero of Daniel's planned novel: S. Wolfe, an anagram
of Fowles.[3]

Much of this book is comprised of Daniel's remi-
niscences and reflections. Whereas the story-line is
easily outlined, the plot—or arrangement and organi-
zation of the elements of the story—is much more
complex and difficult to describe. It is built largely on
flashbacks to, and meditations upon, crucial figures
and episodes in Daniel's life story. It thus calls our
attention, as does the fiction of James Joyce or William
Faulkner, to the arbitrary split of past, present, and

future times. The past is always present in the mind
of Daniel Martin. It is continually being evaluated,
impinging upon the here and now, shaping a future
life.

Equally significant are the shifts in the narrative
perspectives of the story. Included in the novel are
three chapters related from Jenny's point of view, providing the first female narrative voice in Fowles's work
since *The Collector*, and redressing the evident imbalance arising from the otherwise entirely male perceptions. Daniel's own narration is delivered in both
the first and third persons, exemplifying the partial
personae of the man attempting to see himself as
others do by "escap[ing] the first person and be-
com[ing] one's own third."

A more detailed look at the first few chapters
should help to clarify these general observations. The
opening three chapters are third-person accounts, all
of the past, but not in chronological sequence. The
first, entitled "The Harvest" and dated August 1942,
describes in realistic detail a Devon wheat harvest
followed by a massacre of rabbits. It is clear that
Daniel is depicted as a teenager here. At the end of
the chapter, however, there occurs the first incidence
of the characteristic switch in narrative voice and the
subsequent merging of the times and persons comprising the figure of Daniel Martin:

I [the narrator] feel in his [the teenager's] pocket and
bring out a clasp-knife; plunge the blade in the red earth
to clean it of the filth from the two rabbits he has gutted;
slit; liver, intestines, stench. He stands and turns and
begins to carve his initials on the beech-tree. Deep inci-
sions in the bark, peeling the gray skin away to the sappy
green of the living stem. Adieu, my boyhood and my
dream.

Without interfering with its surface realism, Fowles
has provided this scene of harvest and slaughter with

consistent ritualistic and mythic overtones. Along with the exquisite and flawless description of Daniel's adolescent sexual initiation, in a later chapter entitled "Phillida," this first scene establishes the pastoral background to Daniel's reconstructed life. It presents the strategic territory on what is later described as "that emotion-charged map of childhood and adolescence we carry round with us in later life." Daniel will return to the place in his mind, and its images will recur in his narrative. When his daughter, Caroline, is only a few years younger than he was then, he will revisit the place in actuality, and purchase it at auction.

The next chapter, "Games," is set in Los Angeles, in 1977, just before Daniel's departure. By now he is "in ruins," homeless, playing the role of the glib and artificial filmscript writer. The social posturing is epitomized in the title. The third chapter, "The Woman in the Reeds," is set in Oxford during the post-war period. Daniel here is very close to Nicholas Urfe, "the bohemian, the effete middle-class aesthete." Jane and he stumble upon the naked body of a drowned woman, an incident, like the slaughter of the rabbits, that haunts the later narrative. The fourth chapter, "An Unbiased View," is Jenny's first account of him. The one after this, a telephone conversation between Daniel and Jane concerning Anthony's death-bed request, is meant, chronologically and situationally, to continue directly from "Games." The sixth, "Aftermath," set in Daniel's Oxford digs, is the aftermath (a few hours later) of the discovery of the woman in the reeds, and it contains Daniel and Jane's mutual confession of love. This scene is concluded three chapters later, in their "gratuitous act" of love. Their sexual union forms the central event in the collective past of the four friends, the experience that, as Daniel later says, "did not want to die."

One of the principal effects of the style and struc-

ture is to present vividly the fragmentation of the protagonist's life, and our contemporary, "mid-Atlantic"
homelessness more generally. Another is to impress
upon us the manner in which the episodes and the
voices eventually fit together because of the meaningful design that Daniel can make of them. The movement of the plot is clear in this respect: from fragmentation to integration. The last section of the novel
is a chronological account of Daniel and Jane's journey to the Middle East and their return to England,
reflecting the making whole of the central characters.
This emergent pattern is suggested from the outset by
the epigraph to the novel from Antonio Gramsci's
Prison Notebooks: "The crisis consists precisely in the
fact that the old is dying and the new cannot be born;
in this interregnum a great variety of morbid symptoms appears."

In many respects, *Daniel Martin* displays variations on the characters, situations, and themes of
Fowles's earlier works. The figure of Daniel Martin
may be viewed as Nicholas Urfe matured and human-
ized, and each of these protagonists may be seen to
reflect aspects of Fowles's own development as an
author and an individual. Jane and Nell (known at
Oxford as "the Heavenly Twins") reflect Fowles's continuing interest in twins or female pairs, exemplified
previously by the sisters in *The Magus* and "The
Cloud," the two Sarahs in *The French Lieutenant's
Woman,* and the pair of friends in "The Ebony Tower."
Jane herself is an older variation on the attractive and
enigmatic "mystery woman" of the Fowles canon. As
with *The Magus* and *The French Lieutenant's Woman,*
Daniel Martin is centrally concerned with the forma-
tion and destruction of life patterns; with the discov-
eries, the losses, and rediscoveries that are part of the
self-conscious quest for authenticity. Other themes
from *The Aristos* and the fiction are reworked and

developed, especially those related to love, the nature of art, and the novel as a literary form (here mainly discussed in terms of the differences between film and fiction, between screen image and printed word).

Still, *Daniel Martin*, in other respects, represents a milestone in Fowles's fiction writing, a significant maturity of vision and inclusiveness of perspective. To begin with, it is obvious but nonetheless important that Daniel and Jane are his first middle-aged protagonists. Their destinies are charted neither in isolation (as is the case with the characters in *The Collector* and *The Magus*), nor merely against the backdrop of their times (as in *The French Lieutenant's Woman*). Rather, Daniel and Jane are placed in the midst of their fellow human beings, seen in relationship to their families, and as part of their generation, their nation, and their culture. Their portraits are sculptured fully in the round, in detail and without caricature or hyperbole. They are Fowles's most fully realized lovers, the characters most closely approximating live human beings.

Daniel is Fowles's first mature hero, the first to have lived long enough and intensely enough to have grown patient, forgiving, and fair-minded. He is as observant, erudite, cultured, and didactic a man as his creator. Though critical of his age and of his acquaintances, he is nevertheless acutely sensitive to the inevitable imperfections of all human beings and in all human endeavors.

Fowles's previous novels have primarily depicted sexual encounters and power struggles between men and women. They have not dealt nearly as extensively as this one does with the affairs of the heart more generally. This is the first of Fowles's love stories— and let it not be forgotten that *Daniel Martin* is fundamentally a love story—in which the romantic affair plays a secondary role. While an impressive array of sexual relationships is described with considerable frankness in *Daniel Martin*, it is nonetheless true that sexual love is treated in the novel as but one aspect of human love.

This is Fowles's first novel to deal with friendship. It is his first novel to explore familial love—and not just the problems of estrangement and divorce, though these are certainly plotted at length. The relationship of Daniel and Jane is not primarily erotic, albeit its sexual consummations form two of the key scenes of the book. Their relationship is founded on compassion, respect, and the sincere desire for a shared life. *Daniel Martin* is Fowles's first novel with a genuine and satisfying resolution at its end, a real harmonizing of wills, a marriage of true minds.

Nowhere in his previous fiction has Fowles attended to the emotions of children and the responsibilities of parenthood. On the contrary, the parents of his previous heroes and heroines have been either absent or dead; and none of his protagonists, excepting the French Lieutenant's Woman, has offspring of his or her own. In *Daniel Martin*, Fowles explores the relationship of parent and child, especially through Jane and her children, Paul and Rosamund, and through Daniel's renewed intimacy with Caroline. The bond between father and daughter is established slowly, credibly, and movingly; it is developed in depth and with sensitivity.

Other interests, present but not stressed in his earlier fiction, emerge as major fields of discourse in *Daniel Martin*. Since his first draft of *The Magus*, Fowles had meant to write more on his own generation, the generation that reached its majority during the first years of peace after World War II. He describes it in *Daniel Martin* as the "age of self," of "overweening narcissism" and "self-obsession." He focuses on the souring of the Oxford generation of the late 1940s and early 1950s, the wasted potential, the evident underachievement, the failure of nerve. Theirs was a generation driven "into a world with a ubiquitous and insatiable greed for the ephemeral," where the "glamorization of the worthless, the flagrant prostitution of true human values, the substitution of degree of exposure for degree of actual achievement" seemed the norm, not the exception.

Much of this is particularized in Daniel's capitulation to the aesthetic and moral standards of Hollywood. The lost hopes and ambitions of many of the characters in *Daniel Martin* are supposed to account for why "so many became journalists, critics, media men, producers and directors; grew so scared of their pasts and their social class, and never recovered." That Daniel has managed finally to tell his story, to reveal the struggles and decisions and mistakes that have made him what he is, is meant to indicate that he, at least, has recovered.

Another subject emerging as a major and explicit theme in *Daniel Martin* is that of Englishness. In the same radio interview mentioned earlier, Fowles characterizes this novel as a "long essay on Englishness," on "what it is to be English." In *The Magus*, Nicholas's national characteristics are occasionally contrasted with those of the Greeks. Here the contrast, between the English and the Americans, is developed in depth, although it is all too evident that Fowles knows the English better than the Americans, and Oxford more intimately than Hollywood.

The genesis of his remarks on the English character in *Daniel Martin* is to be found in a little-known and very early essay of his, "On Being English but Not British."[4] In the essay and the novel (especially the chapter called "The Sacred Combe"), Fowles claims that the quintessential English myth is that of Robin Hood. By this he means to epitomize the English predisposition for seclusion, the behavior pattern in which the true self is revealed only in private (in the greenwood, as it were) and allowed to emerge in broad daylight (under the scrutiny of the nasty Sheriff of Nottingham) only in disguise. According to Fowles, this national characteristic of withdrawal, of hiding the emotions behind the public mask, allows for a singularly English self-consciousness, self-criticism, and tolerance. It also accounts, he thinks, for the distinctive ways in which the English use language, especially in contrast to Americans.

Finally, *Daniel Martin* is, by far, the most compassionate book Fowles has written. It was Fowles's declared intention (also in that same radio interview) to suggest a "humanist point of view of life." As it is most often used today, the term *humanism* refers both to the welfare of humanity and to the humanities. Fowles must surely have had the double reference in mind. The last page of the novel describes Daniel's meditation before a late Rembrandt self-portrait. The gaze of the old artist from the canvas gives Daniel the secret he has been searching for: "choosing and learning to feel." The "ultimate citadel of humanism" lies in the knowledge that there is "no true compassion without will, no true will without compassion." Having arrived at the end of this long journey of a book, Fowles's readers are able to understand its implied last sentence, the sentence that is also its explicit first: "Whole sight; or all the rest is desolation."

Mirroring Fowles's novelistic habit, it is perhaps fitting that this monograph conclude with the fresh beginning that *Daniel Martin* seems to represent. That it received mixed reviews is not surprising as it could never be a novel for everyone. John Gardner, himself the distinguished author of eight novels, reviewed *Daniel Martin* in superlative terms. Overlooking John Barth, Patrick White, Saul Bellow, and other candi-

120 John Fowles

dates, Gardner extols John Fowles as "the only novelist now writing in English whose works are likely to
stand as literary classics—the only writer in English
who has the power, range, knowledge, and wisdom of
a Tolstoi or James."[5] Perhaps Gardner's estimation is
but another instance of the tendency toward exaggera-
tion among Fowles's admirers (a characteristic, incidentally, also inspired by James and Tolstoi). The
power of his narrative art, the range of his subject
matter, and his personal erudition, however, are evident in each of Fowles's major works. Perhaps the new
insistence in *Daniel Martin* on compassion and whole
sight is the first step of this master stylist on the road
to wisdom.

Notes

1. Introduction

1. John Fowles, *The Aristos,* rev. ed. (New York: New American Library, Signet, 1970), p. 7.
2. John Fowles, "My Recollections of Kafka," *Mosaic* 4 (Summer 1970): 31-41.
3. *Current Biography* 38 (March 1977): 14.
4. The first stage version of *The Collector* was done in French: *L'obsédé,* by France Roche, at Théâtre des Variétés, in November 1966. An English dramatization by David Parker was first produced at the King's Head Theatre Club, Islington, in February 1971, and the acting edition published by Samuel French in 1973.
5. Roy Newquist, "John Fowles," in *Counterpoint* (Chicago: Rand McNally, 1964), p. 222.
6. *World Authors, 1950-1970,* ed. John Wakeman (New York: H. W. Wilson, 1975), p. 485.
7. *The Aristos* (Boston: Little, Brown and Co., 1964), p. 166.
8. See, for example, Fowles's introduction to Sabine Baring-Gould's *Mehalah* (London: Chatto and Windus, 1969) and his foreword to Piers Brendon's *Hawker of Morwenstow* (London: Jonathan Cape, 1975). In both he discusses his attraction to courageous and eccentric personalities.
9. "Letter from the Publisher," *Sports Illustrated,* December 1970, p. 5. This provides an introduction to Fowles's curious piece on conservation in the same issue of *Sports Illustrated,* entitled "Weeds, Bugs, Americans."

10. Mark Amory, "Tales out of School," *Sunday Times Magazine*, 22 September 1974, p. 33.

11. *World Authors, 1950-1970*, pp. 485-486.

12. *The Aristos* (1964), p. 9.

13. Richard Boston, "John Fowles, Alone but Not Lonely," *New York Times Book Review*, 9 November 1969, p. 52.

14. *World Authors, 1950-1970*, p. 486.

15. John Fowles, "Notes on an Unfinished Novel," in *Afterwords; Novelists on their Novels*, ed. Thomas McCormack (New York: Harper and Row, 1969), p. 173. These "Notes" first appeared in a slightly abbreviated form in "Notes on Writing a Novel," *Harper's Magazine*, July 1968.

16. "Notes on an Unfinished Novel," p. 173.

17. Richard B. Stolley, "The French Lieutenant's Woman's Man, Novelist John Fowles," *Life* 68 (29 May 1970): 57.

18. "Imminent Victorians" [rv. of *The French Lieutenant's Woman*], *Time* (7 November 1969): 108.

19. "Notes on an Unfinished Novel," pp. 161-162.

20. Newquist, "John Fowles," in *Counterpoint*, pp. 222 and 220.

21. Daniel Halpern, "A Sort of Exile in Lyme Regis," *London Magazine*, March 1971, p. 45.

22. *The Aristos*, p. 14.

23. *The Aristos*, p. 209.

24. *The Aristos*, pp. 137-138.

25. In a letter to George and Tom Keats, 21 December 1817. In *The Letters of John Keats*, ed. Hyder E. Rollins (Cambridge: Harvard University Press, 1958), I, 193.

26. *The Aristos*, p. 226.

27. *The Aristos*, p. 214.

28. See, for example, Fowles's articles entitled "The Trouble with Starlets," *Holiday* 39 (June 1966): 12-20; and "Jacqueline Kennedy Onassis and Other First (and Last) Ladies," *Cosmopolitan* 170 (October 1970): 144-149.

2. *The Collector*

1. *The Aristos,* rev. ed. (New York: New American Library, Signet, 1970), p. 124.
2. Roy Newquist, "John Fowles," in *Counterpoint* (Chicago: Rand McNally, 1964), p. 219.
3. Preface to rev. ed. of *The Aristos,* p. 10.
4. I learned of this alteration in the manuscript of *The Collector* from Fowles himself, in an interview in Lyme Regis, 29 August 1977.
5. Newquist, "John Fowles," p. 218; and preface to rev. ed. of *The Aristos,* pp. 10-11.
6. A useful summary of the characteristics of necrophilia is provided in Erich Fromm, *The Anatomy of Human Destructiveness* (New York: Holt, Rinehart and Winston, 1973), ch. 12.

3. *The Magus*

1. *The Aristos,* rev. ed. (New York: New American Library, Signet, 1970), pp. 213 and 175.
2. John Fowles, "*The Magus* Revisited," *The Times,* 28 May 1977, p. 7.
3. Richard Boston, "John Fowles, Alone but Not Lonely," *New York Times Book Review,* 9 November 1969, p. 2.
4. Daniel Halpern, "A Sort of Exile in Lyme Regis," *London Magazine* 10 (March 1971): 35.
5. "A Sort of Exile in Lyme Regis," p. 35. Fowles expands upon the genesis of *The Magus* and the various influences upon him at the time of writing in the foreword to the revised version.
6. In a personal interview at Lyme Regis, 29 August 1977.
7. First observed by Robert Scholes, "The Orgastic Fiction of John Fowles," *Hollins Critic* 6 (December 1969): 4. The relationship between ethics and aesthetics, Scholes believes, is the central concern of the novel.

8. So identified by Fowles himself, in *Poems* (New York: Ecco Press, 1973), p. 2. See also Robert H. Pilpel, who, probably unaware of Fowles's identification of the place, set out to "discover" it, and records his journey and his findings in "The Isle of the Magus," *New York Sunday Times*, 24 August 1975, sec. 10.

9. Boston, "John Fowles, Alone but Not Lonely," p. 2.

10. Lorna Sage, "Profile 7: John Fowles," *New Review* 1 (October 1974): 33.

11. Fowles, "My Recollections of Kafka," *Mosaic* 4 (Summer 1970): 37.

12. Arthur Edward Waite, *The Pictorial Key to the Tarot* (1910; rpt. New York: University Books, 1959), p. 155.

13. For an enlargement of this approach, see P. D. Ouspensky, *A New Model of the Universe*, 3rd ed. (London: Routledge and Kegan Paul, 1938), ch. V ("The Symbolism of the Tarot").

14. Thomas Churchill, "Waterhouse, Storey, and Fowles: Which Way out of the Room?" *Critique* 10 (1969): 87.

15. Richard B. Stolley, "The French Lieutenant's Woman's Man, Novelist John Fowles," *Life* 68 (29 May 1970): 60.

16. E. M. Forster, *Aspects of the Novel* (London: Edward Arnold, 1927), p. 216.

17. Martin Shuttleworth, "New Novels," *Punch* 250 (4 May 1966): 668.

4. *The French Lieutenant's Woman*

1. *The Aristos* (Boston: Little, Brown, 1964), p. 93.

2. David North, "Interview with Author John Fowles," *Maclean's* 90 (14 November 1977): 8.

3. The parallels with Victorian literature remain largely beyond the scope of this study, though from time to time specific references to Victorian literature will be made. Much of the academic criticism and many of

the reviews of *The French Lieutenant's Woman* deal
with Fowles's debt to the nineteenth-century poets
and novelists, and with the use he makes of their
stylistic conventions. The interested reader is referred
to the bibliography for the important articles and to
Note 6 below, which outlines the literature on
Fowles's supposed debt to Thomas Hardy. Finally, I
should mention here that Fowles, in his introduction
to his translation of Claire de Durfort's *Ourika*
(Austin, Texas: W. Thomas Taylor, 1977), claims
only recently to have perceived that the principal
literary ancestor of the French Lieutenant's Woman
is the eponymous heroine of *Ourika*. Like Sarah
Woodruff, Ourika is an outsider, isolated from her
"natural kind" by breeding and intelligence. She is
in love with, but cannot marry, an aristocrat named
Charles, also the name of the aristocratic hero of *The
French Lieutenant's Woman.*

4. G. M. Young, *Victorian England: Portrait of an Age,*
    2nd ed. (London: Oxford University Press, 1953),
    p. 181.

5. Fowles, "Notes on an Unfinished Novel," in *After-
    words: Novelists on Their Novels,* ed. Thomas Mc-
    Cormack (New York: Harper and Row, 1969), p.
    171. These "Notes," already quoted at length in the
    Introduction, were written concurrently with *The
    French Lieutenant's Woman* and are especially inter-
    esting for the light they shed on the genesis and
    development of the novel. A similar acknowledge-
    ment to Hardy can be found at the end of chapter
    35 of the novel.

6. Walter Allen has called Sarah "a figure out of a
    Hardy ballad" ("The Achievement of John Fowles,"
    Encounter, August 1970, p. 66). Jeff Rackham, "John
    Fowles: the Existential Labyrinth," *Critique* 13
    (1972): 100, points to Grace Melbury in *The Wood-
    landers* as Sarah's closest literary antecedent. Fred
    Kaplan, "Victorian Modernists: Fowles and Nabo-
    kov," *Journal of Narrative Technique* 3 (May 1973):
    111, points to Tess and Sue Bridehead (as well as

Dickens's Miss Wade and Eliot's Dorothea Brooke) as her literary forebears. The most elaborate source study in this respect is that of A. A. De Vitis and William J. Palmer, "A Pair of Blue Eyes Flash at the French Lieutenant's Woman," *Contemporary Literature* 15 (Winter 1974): 90-101, in which it is argued that Hardy's *A Pair of Blue Eyes* provided a major source of inspiration for Fowles, evident in plot, theme, image patterns, and characterization. Especially significant are the parallel relationships of Fowles's Charles and Sarah and Hardy's Stephen Smith and Elfride Swancourt. Both couples, the authors argue, reflect Hardy's own tragic love affair with his supposed cousin Tryphena, to which Fowles makes reference in *The French Lieutenant's Woman*.

7. "Notes on an Unfinished Novel," p. 165.

8. In a recent letter to me, Fowles mentioned that Sarah was intended physically to recall Elizabeth Siddal, the favorite model of the Pre-Raphaelite Brotherhood. Again I regret that the scope of this study will not allow for more detailed comparison with the unconventional pictorial art of the period, a comparison which would certainly shed light on the mysterious appeal of Sarah Woodruff and on the craft of her creator. William Holman Hunt's two-volume *Pre-Raphaelitism and the Pre-Raphaelite Brotherhood* (1905) is the monumental contemporary account of the movement. Two recent books on the Pre-Raphaelites and their influence on *fin de siècle* art, both with chapters devoted to the new ideal of feminine beauty, are: John Dixon Hunt, *The Pre-Raphaelite Imagination, 1848-1900* (London: Routledge and Kegan Paul, 1968); Philippe Julian, *Dreamers of Decadence: Symbolist Painters of the 1890s,* trans. Robert Baldick (New York: Praeger, 1971), originally published in 1969 as *Esthetes et Magiciens.*

9. Jeff Rackham, "John Fowles: The Existential Labyrinth," *Critique* 13 (1972): 100-101.

10. For a fuller exposition of the development of this

pattern of imagery, see Elizabeth D. Rankin, "Cryptic Coloration in *The French Lieutenant's Woman*," *Journal of Narrative Technique* 3 (September 1973): 199-201.

11. Fowles, "Foreword," *Poems* (New York: Ecco Press, 1973), p. vii.

12. There are two especially relevant novels that should be noted here. One, itself an experimental work, is Anthony Froude's *The Lieutenant's Daughter* (1847). This contains alternative endings, and it is convincingly discussed as a possible literary progenitor to *The French Lieutenant's Woman* by Phyllis Grosskurth, "*The French Lieutenant's Woman*," *Victorian Studies* 16 (September 1972): 130-131. The other is Dickens's *Great Expectations*, a novel that had already exerted an influence on *The Magus* (see Fowles's Foreword to the revised version). Christopher Ricks, in his review of *The French Lieutenant's Woman*, *New York Review of Books*, 12 February 1970, p. 24, treats the endings of *The French Lieutenant's Woman* as "an adaptation of the famous *Great Expectations* crux." In Dickens's original ending, the hero gains only a glimpse of his beloved, while, in the revised ending, he gains the lady herself.

13. David Lodge, "*The Novelist at the Crossroads*" *and Other Essays on Fiction and Criticism* (Ithaca: Cornell University Press, 1971), p. 18.

5.   *The Ebony Tower*

1. *The Aristos*, rev. ed., p. 197.

2. David North, "Interview with Author John Fowles," *Maclean's* 90 (14 November 1977): 6; and John F. Baker, "John Fowles," *Publisher's Weekly* 206 (25 November 1974): 6.

3. Theodore Solotaroff, "John Fowles's Linear Art," *New York Times Book Review*, 10 November 1974, p. 2.

4. First noted by Constance B. Hieatt, "*Eliduc* Revis-

ited: John Fowles and Marie de France," *English Studies in Canada* 3 (Fall 1977): 357.

5. Peter Prince, "Real Life," *New Statesman* 88 (11 October 1974): 513.

6. Lorna Sage, "Profile 7: John Fowles," *New Review* 1 (October 1974): 37.

7. Solotaroff, "John Fowles's Linear Art," p. 3.

8. Baker, "John Fowles," p. 7.

9. Baker, "John Fowles," p. 7.

6. *Daniel Martin*

1. Fowles, "I Write Therefore I Am," *Evergreen Review* 8 (August-September 1964): 90.

2. Interview with Eric Friesen, CBC Radio, 30 September 1977.

3. Mentioned in a paper by David H. Walker, "Subversion of Narrative in the Work of André Gide and John Fowles: from Ironic Monologue to Self-Conscious Novel," delivered to the annual conference of the British Comparative Literature Association, in December 1977. Mr. Walker was kind enough to send me a copy of the typescript of his paper.

4. Fowles, "On Being English but Not British," *Texas Quarterly* 7 (Autumn 1964): 154-162.

5. John Gardner, "In Defense of the Real," *Saturday Review*, 1 October 1977, p. 22.

Bibliography

I. Works by John Fowles: Books

The Aristos: A Self-Portrait in Ideas. Boston: Little, Brown and Co., 1964; London: Jonathan Cape, 1965.

The Aristos, rev. ed. London: Pan Books, 1968; Boston: Little, Brown and Co., 1970.

The Collector. London: Jonathan Cape, 1963; Boston: Little, Brown and Co., 1963.

Daniel Martin. London: Jonathan Cape, 1977; Boston: Little, Brown and Co., 1977; Toronto: Collins, 1977.

The Ebony Tower. London: Jonathan Cape, 1974; Boston: Little, Brown and Co., 1974.

The French Lieutenant's Woman. London: Jonathan Cape, 1969; Boston: Little, Brown and Co., 1969.

The Magus. Boston: Little, Brown and Co., 1965; London: Jonathan Cape, 1966.

The Magus, rev. ed. with Foreword. London: Jonathan Cape, 1977; Boston: Little, Brown and Co., 1978.

Poems. New York: Ecco Press, 1973; Toronto: Macmillan, 1973.

Shipwreck, text by Fowles, photography by the Gibsons of Scilly. London: Jonathan Cape, 1974; Boston: Little, Brown and Co., 1975.

II. Works by John Fowles: Other Writings

Afterword to *The Wanderer, Or the End of Youth*, by Alain-Fournier, trans. Lowell Bair. New York: New American Library, Signet, 1971.

Durfort, Claire de. *Ourika* (1824). Translated with Introduction and Epilogue by Fowles. Austin, Texas: W.
Thomas Taylor, 1977. Limited handset edition of
500 copies.

Foreword to *Hawker of Morwenstow: Portrait of a Victorian Eccentric*, by Piers Brendon. London: Jonathan
Cape, 1975.

Foreword and Afterword to *The Hound of the Baskervilles*,
by Sir Arthur Conan Doyle. London: John Murray
and Jonathan Cape, 1974.

"I Write Therefore I Am." *Evergreen Review* 8 (August-
September 1964): 16-17, 89-90.

"In Paradise." *Transatlantic Review* 14 (Autumn 1963):
9-15.

Introduction, Glossary, and Appendix to *Mehalah, a Story
of the Salt Marshes* (1880), by Sabine Baring-Gould.
London: Chatto and Windus, 1969.

"Is the Novel Dead?" *Books*, Autumn 1970, pp. 2-5.

"Jacqueline Kennedy Onassis and Other First (and Last)
Ladies." *Cosmopolitan* 170 (October 1970): 144-149.

"The Magus Revisited." London *Times*, 28 May 1977, p. 7.

"Making a Pitch for Cricket." *Sports Illustrated* 38 (21
May 1973): 100-114.

"My Recollections of Kafka." *Mosaic* 4 (Summer 1970):
31-41.

"Notes on Writing a Novel." *Harper's Magazine* 237 (July
1968): 88-97. Reprinted with emendations and additions as: "On Writing a Novel," *Cornhill Magazine*,
Summer 1969, pp. 281-295; "Notes on an Unfinished
Novel," in *Afterwords: Novelists on their Novels*, ed.
Thomas McCormack. New York: Harper and Row,
1969; "Notes on an Unfinished Novel," in *The Novel
Today: Contemporary Writers on Modern Fiction*, ed.
Malcolm Bradbury. Manchester: Manchester University Press, 1977 and London: Fontana/Collins,
1977.

"Of Memoirs and Magpies." *Atlantic* 235 (June 1975):
82-84.

"On Being English but Not British." *Texas Quarterly* 7
(Autumn 1964): 154-162.

"Party of One: The Trouble with Starlets." *Holiday* 39 (June 1966): 12-20.

Perrault, Charles. *Cinderella* (1697). Adapted and translated by Fowles, illustrated by Sheilah Beckett. Boston: Little, Brown and Co., 1974.

"Weeds, Bugs, Americans." *Sports Illustrated*, December 1970, pp. 84-102.

III. WORKS ABOUT JOHN FOWLES

Adam, Ian; Brantlinger, Patrick; and Rothblatt, Sheldon. "*The French Lieutenant's Woman:* A Discussion." *Victorian Studies* 15 (March 1972): 339-356.

Allen, Walter. "The Achievement of John Fowles." *Encounter*, August 1970, pp. 64-67.

Amory, Mark. "Tales out of School." London *Sunday Times Magazine*, 22 September 1974, pp. 33, 34, 36.

Baker, John F. "John Fowles." *Publisher's Weekly* 206 (25 November 1974): 6-7.

Berets, Ralph. "*The Magus:* A Study in the Creation of a Personal Myth." *Twentieth Century Literature* 19 (April 1973): 89-98.

Binns, Ronald. "John Fowles: Radical Romancer." *Critical Quarterly* 15 (Winter 1973): 317-334.

Boston, Richard. "John Fowles, Alone but Not Lonely." *New York Times Book Review*, 9 November 1969, pp. 2, 52, 53.

Bradbury, Malcolm. "John Fowles's *The Magus*." In *Sense and Sensibility in Twentieth-Century Writing; a Gathering in Memory of William Van O'Connor*, edited by Brom Weber. Carbondale, Illinois: Southern Illinois University Press, 1970. Reprinted as "The Novelist as Impresario: John Fowles and His Magus." In *Possibilities: Essays on the State of the Novel*, by Malcolm Bradbury. London: Oxford University Press, 1973.

Campbell, James. "An Interview with John Fowles." *Contemporary Literature* 17 (Autumn 1976): 455-469.

Churchill, Thomas. "Waterhouse, Storey, and Fowles:

Which Way out of the Room?" *Critique* 10 (1969): 72-87.

Corbett, Thomas. "The Film and the Book: A Case Study of *The Collector.*" *English Journal* 57 (March 1968): 328-333.

Costa, Richard Hauer. "Trickery's Mixed Bag: The Perils of Fowles' *French Lieutenant's Woman.*" *Rocky Mountain Review of Language and Literature* 29 (Spring 1975): 1-9.

DeVitis, A. A., and Palmer, William J. "A Pair of Blue Eyes Flash at the French Lieutenant's Woman." *Contemporary Literature* 15 (Winter 1974): 90-101.

Eddins, Dwight. "John Fowles: Existence as Authorship." *Contemporary Literature* 17 (Spring 1976): 204-222.

Edwards, Lee R. "Changing our Imaginations." *Massachusetts Review* 11 (1970): 604-608.

Evarts, Prescott, Jr. "Fowles' *The French Lieutenant's Woman* as Tragedy." *Critique* 13 (1972): 57-69.

————. "John Fowles: A Checklist." *Critique* 13 (1972): 105-107.

Fleishman, Avrom. "*The Magus* of the Wizard of the West." *Journal of Modern Literature* 5 (April 1976): 297-314.

"Fowles, John." In *Current Biography* 38 (March 1977): 11-15.

"Fowles, John." In *World Authors, 1950-1970.* Edited by John Wakeman. New York: H. W. Wilson, 1975.

Gardner, John. "In Defense of the Real" [review of *Daniel Martin*]. *Saturday Review,* 1 October 1977, pp. 22-24.

Grosskurth, Phyllis. "*The French Lieutenant's Woman.*" *Victorian Studies* 16 (September 1972): 130-131.

Gussow, Mel. "Talk with John Fowles." *New York Times Book Review,* 13 November 1977, pp. 3, 84, 85.

Halpern, Daniel. "A Sort of Exile in Lyme Regis." *London Magazine,* March 1971, pp. 34-46.

Hieatt, Constance B. "*Eliduc* Revisited: John Fowles and Marie de France." *English Studies in Canada* 3 (Fall 1977): 351-358.

Kaplan, Fred. "Victorian Modernists: Fowles and Nabokov." *Journal of Narrative Technique* 3 (1973): 108-120.

Kennedy, Alan. "John Fowles's Sense of an Ending" (ch. 7). In his *The Protean Self: Dramatic Action in Contemporary Fiction*. London: Macmillan, 1974.

Laughlin, Rosemary M. "Faces of Power in the Novels of John Fowles." *Critique* 13 (1972): 71-88.

Mellors, John. "Collectors and Creators: the Novels of John Fowles." *London Magazine* 14 (February/March 1975): 65-72.

Myers, Karen Magee. "John Fowles: An Annotated Bibliography, 1963-1976." *Bulletin of Bibliography and Magazine Notes* 33 (Summer 1976): 162-169.

Newquist, Roy. "John Fowles." In his *Counterpoint*. Chicago: Rand McNally, 1964, pp. 218-225.

North, David. "Interview with Author John Fowles." *Maclean's* 90 (14 November 1977): 4, 6, 8.

Olshen, Barry N. "John Fowles's *The Magus:* An Allegory of Self-Realization." *Journal of Popular Culture* 9 (Spring 1976): 916-925.

Palmer, William J. *The Fiction of John Fowles: Tradition, Art, and the Loneliness of Selfhood*. Columbia, Missouri: University of Missouri Press, Literary Frontiers Edition, 1974.

Presley, Delma E. "The Quest of the Bourgeois Hero: An Approach to Fowles' *The Magus*." *Journal of Popular Culture* 6 (Fall 1972): 394-398.

Pritchard, William H. "An English Hero" [review of *Daniel Martin*]. *New York Times Book Review*, 25 September 1977, pp. 1 and 42.

Rackham, Jeff. "John Fowles: The Existential Labyrinth." *Critique* 13 (1972): 89-103.

Rankin, Elizabeth D. "Cryptic Coloration in *The French Lieutenant's Woman*." *Journal of Narrative Technique* 3 (September 1973): 193-207.

Rose, Gilbert J. "*The French Lieutenant's Woman:* The Unconscious Significance of a Novel to its Author." *American Imago* 29 (Summer 1972): 165-176.

Rubenstein, Roberta. "Myth, Mystery, and Irony: John

Fowles's *The Magus.*" *Contemporary Literature* 16 (Summer 1975): 328-339.

Sage, Lorna. "Profile 7: John Fowles." *New Review* 1 (October 1974): 31-37.

Scholes, Robert. "The Orgastic Fiction of John Fowles." *Hollins Critic* 6 (December 1969): 1-12.

Solotaroff, Theodore. "John Fowles's Linear Art" [review of *The Ebony Tower*]. *New York Times Book Review,* 10 November 1974, pp. 2, 3, 20.

Stolley, Richard B. "The French Lieutenant's Woman's Man: Novelist John Fowles." *Life* 68 (29 May 1970): 55-60.

Tatham, Michael. "Two Novels: Notes on the Work of John Fowles." *New Blackfriars* 52 (September 1971): 404-411.

Watt, Ian. "A Traditional Victorian Novel? Yes, and Yet . . ." [review of *The French Lieutenant's Woman*]. *New York Times Book Review,* 9 November 1969, pp. 1, 74, 75.

Wolfe, Peter. *John Fowles, Magus and Moralist.* Lewisburg, Pa.: Bucknell University Press, 1976; London: Associated University Presses, 1976.

Index